watch your mouth

TONY EVANS

HARVEST HOUSE PUBLISHERS
EUGENE, OREGON

Cover by Troy Black

WATCH YOUR MOUTH
Copyright © 2016 Tony Evans
Published by Harvest House Publishers
Eugene, Oregon 97402
www.harvesthousepublishers.com

ISBN 978-0-7369-6060-1 (pbk.)
ISBN 978-0-7369-6061-8 (eBook)

Library of Congress Cataloging-in-Publication Data
Names: Evans, Tony, 1949- author.
Title: Watch your mouth / Tony Evans.
Description: Eugene, Oregon : Harvest House Publishers, 2016.
Identifiers: LCCN 2016000195 (print) | LCCN 2016004707 (ebook) | ISBN
    9780736960601 (pbk.) | ISBN 9780736960618 ()
Subjects: LCSH: Oral communication—Religious aspects—Christianity. |
    Rhetoric—Religious aspects—Christianity. | Language and
    languages—Religious aspects—Christianity. | Mouth—Miscellanea.
Classification: LCC BV4597.53.C64 E93 2016 (print) | LCC BV4597.53.C64
    (ebook) | DDC 241/.672—dc23
LC record available at http://lccn.loc.gov/2016000195

Printed in the United States of America

16 17 18 19 20 21 22 23 24 / BP-CD / 10 9 8 7 6 5 4 3

contents

Introduction

A Greek philosopher once invited some very influential and powerful guests to his home for dinner two nights in a row. He told them he was going to provide them with the best possible meal on the first night and the worst possible meal on the second night.

When his guests arrived, the servant set before them a meal of smothered tongue. The guests asked why this would be considered the best possible meal.

The philosopher replied, "The tongue is what we use to bless people, communicate happiness, dispel sorrow, and remove despair. We also use it to help the fainthearted, inspire the discouraged, and uplift all mankind. The tongue is the best possible meal."

The next night the guests returned to the philosopher's home for dinner, this time expecting the worst possible meal. Yet once again the servants brought out smothered tongue. The guests were curious why the same entrée was served twice, and they asked how it could be so.

The philosopher replied, "With the tongue we break hearts, bring curses, destroy reputations, promote discord, induce strife, and set wars in motion."

In other words, you can use the very same thing to do good or to do evil. The same tool holds the power to do it all.

I'm sure you've heard the saying, "Sticks and stones may break my bones, but words will never hurt me." That phrase is a lie. At some point in your life, you have undoubtedly been hurt by other people's words. You have most likely also hurt people from time to time with your own words. Proverbs summarizes it this way:

> From the fruit of his mouth a man's stomach is satisfied;
> he is filled with the product of his lips.
> Life and death are in the power of the tongue,
> and those who love it will eat its fruit (Proverbs
>   18:20-21).

The tool behind your teeth, the tongue, can influence your world for good or for bad. It can bring life, or it can bring death.

The mouth and the tongue not only take things in but also produce things that come out. It goes in both directions. Your words will provide a helping of life or a helping of death because life and death are in the power of the tongue.

Words matter much more than most people realize. History was inaugurated with divine speech as God brought creation into existence through His words. So it should not surprise us that when the triune God created mankind in His image, speech was a part of the package. He intended humankind not only to communicate with Him, but also with each other on His behalf.

Human speech was also designed not only to communicate the intentions of our mind and heart, but also to carry the power and authority to bring into reality the will of God. This is why the Bible says that when Adam named the animals God brought before him, "whatever [Adam] called a living creature, that was its name" (Genesis 2:19). God recognizes, validates, and empoweres speech that is consistent with His will. Therefore the words coming out of our mouths are a powerful expression of the image of God at work in our lives.

That's why it should not surprise us that when Satan tempted Eve in the garden, it was not only *with* speech, but it was also *about* speech. The serpent said to the woman, "Did God really say, 'You can't eat from any tree in the garden?'" (Genesis 3:1). Words outside of God's will have a power that leads to death, while the words of God bring creation to life.

The point is simply this: Speech has power and words really do matter. When connected to the word and will of God, our speech brings life, help, and hope to both the speaker and hearer. When disconnected from the Creator of speech, it brings despair, hopelessness, confusion (as at the Tower of Babel—Genesis 11:1-9), and death. Life and death are truly in the power of the tongue.

Power to Heal, Power to Destroy

In the book of Deuteronomy, we read of Moses speaking to the nation of Israel about this reality: "I call heaven and earth as witnesses against you today that I have set before you life and death, blessing and curse. Choose life so that you and your descendants may live" (Deuteronomy 30:19). When Moses says, "life and death," he is not referring to killing people physically. He means they can choose to bring blessing or destruction through their choices, and that would include their choice of words.

Life is the enjoyment of the favor of God. Death is the removal of divine favor, leading to the death of a dream, the death of a relationship, or whatever. The same tool in your mouth can bring both. In a surgeon's skilled hand, a scalpel can help preserve life, but a criminal can use the same sharpened blade to bring death. A wise doctor can use a syringe to promote healing in a sick patient, but a drug pusher can use the same syringe to cause death.

You and I have the power to bring blessing or a curse upon each other and upon ourselves simply through our mouths—the ability to do both is found in it. You don't have to kill a person physically in order to ruin their life forever. Myriads of people have been wiped out by words. Proverbs 6:2 says, "You have been trapped by the words of your lips—ensnared by the words of your mouth." Our words can trap us. They can get us into situations we never should have gotten into. They can bind us in commitments we never should have made. The tongue can heal, or it can harm: "The tongue that heals is a tree of life, but a devious tongue breaks the spirit" (Proverbs 15:4).

Far too many of us use our tongues flippantly to voice how we feel or what we think, but do we use it powerfully? Your tongue is a tool that can create blessing and breathe life—not only for yourself but also for those around you. But keep in mind, your tongue also has the power to bring death. We see both summarized in Proverbs 12:18: "There is one who speaks rashly, like a piercing sword; but the tongue of the wise brings healing." And again in Proverbs 13:3: "The one who guards his mouth protects his life; the one who opens his lips invites his own ruin."

Since your tongue is such an incredibly powerful tool, you can imagine why your mouth is like a battleground between God and the devil. There is a war for your words because through your words come life or death. That's why I took the time to teach through the various aspects of the mouth and wrote about them here for you—so that you will be equipped to use your mouth for good and discern when it could be used for evil.

Nuclear power can be very beneficial. We are able to improve our lives with this form of power by generating electricity, powering huge ships, and so on. Yet a nuclear bomb can also destroy an entire city. It can wipe out life altogether. The same is true for your mouth.

Unfortunately, though, many of us fail to realize how significant our speech really is. And so, over and over and over again, we speak words that bring ill health, death, and destruction. And then we wonder why we are depressed and hurting.

When God wanted to create something, He used words.

Speak life with your lips and watch life come about. When God wanted to create something, He used words. When Satan wanted to destroy something, he used words. Both of them used words in order to exercise their power. If you and I were to change the way we view our mouths and recognize the power of our words, we could literally change our lives for good. Just as you would be careful when handling a loaded gun, you would realize how important it is to be careful with a loaded mouth. You would ask yourself, "Am I bringing favor into this situation, or am I bringing a curse?" And then you would alter your speech accordingly so as to invite favor.

So crucial are our words that the psalmist writes, "LORD, set up a guard for my mouth; keep watch at the door of my lips" (Psalm 141:3). What does a guard do? He or she opens and shuts a door at the appropriate time. Essentially, the psalmist is asking God to station a policeman at the entrance to his mouth. That sentry would let the psalmist know when to speak and when not to.

That's what it means to watch your mouth. Guard it. Police it. It is a powerful tool for both good and evil. Do a favor for yourself and everyone around you by using your mouth for good. Just how to do that is what we're going to be looking at through the pages of this book. I hope you'll be encouraged as much as I was when I studied this topic and prepared these teachings. When used rightly, your mouth is a strong asset in so many ways.

It's like the cowboy who was driving down the highway in his truck with his dog beside him and his horse in a trailer. He hit a corner too hard, and they all flipped. A policeman arrived at the scene shortly after it happened. He approached the horse and saw that it wasn't going to survive, so he sadly put down the horse to relieve it of its pain. Then he examined the dog and saw that it too was in agony and near death, so he put down the dog as well. After that he walked over to the cowboy and asked how he felt.

Seeing the policeman's gun still smoking, the cowboy quickly said, "I ain't never felt better!"

Your words can save your life!

This is why the message of this book is so important. If we can learn to manage our mouths so that our words are strategically linked to God's intended purpose for speech, then we can see His powerful presence change our course as well the course of those in the sphere of our influence. It's time for all of us to take seriously the imperative, *Watch Your Mouth*.

Part 1

the power of the tongue

Dynamite in Your Dentures

In 1866, one invention changed the world forever. That was the year Alfred Nobel developed the first safe but powerful explosive—dynamite.

Until that time, people used either gunpowder or nitroglycerin to build roads or do any other construction project that required an explosive. The problem with gunpowder was its inefficacy—it was not powerful enough to do much except fire a bullet. The problem with nitroglycerine was a lot worse. Any little jiggle or agitation while transporting it (most often in liquid form) would cause an immediate explosion. The slightest spark could set it off without warning. Many construction workers and transportation specialists lost their lives simply by trying to get this flammable and volatile material to its intended destination.

But in 1866, just two years after his younger brother died in an accidental blast of nitroglycerine, Alfred Nobel—a young man fueled by his near obsession to do so—discovered a way to combine

nitroglycerine with a stabilizer, making it nearly impossible to deto-
nate until intentionally triggered.

Alfred Nobel's dynamic invention paved the way for the rapid
advance of the modern culture. Dynamite provided an unprece-
dented amount of safety and ability to develop the infrastructure so
desperately needed.

With the new ease of transportation and usage, Nobel's dynamite
quickly leveled areas where roads needed to be built or expanded. It
provided access to areas that were previously unreachable and blew
through once impenetrable mountainsides. It saved workers' lives
and promoted a greater quality of life for those who benefited from
increased access to goods, services, medicines, and so on.

Nobel's dynamite improved life and society on many levels. But
on the other hand, it also brought destruction. Dynamite quickly
became an accurate and deadly force as a weapon of war. In fact,
Alfred Nobel himself spent a large portion of his time, energy, and
money inventing various weapons that he believed could one day—
due to their deadly effectiveness—end war altogether. He commented to his close friend and confidante, Austrian countess Bertha
von Suttner, "Perhaps my factories will put an end to war sooner than
your congresses: on the day that two army corps can mutually annihi-
late each other in a second, all civilized nations will surely recoil with
horror and disband their troops."[1]

Despite his desire to end war through the creation and refinement
of weaponry, wars only increased. No one knows for certain his motivation, but just a year before he died, Alfred Nobel established the
Nobel Peace Prize in his will. He specified that the annual award was
to go to an individual who had clearly demonstrated "the most or the
best work for fraternity among nations, for the abolition or reduc-
tion of standing armies and for the promotion of peace congresses."

Some speculate Alfred Nobel left his life's legacy of the Nobel

Peace Prize as a way to settle the score because his invention had brought so much destruction. One commented to Albert Einstein during a time of his own reckoning with regard to scientific advances that "Alfred Nobel invented an explosive more powerful than any then known—an exceedingly effective means of destruction. To atone for this 'accomplishment' and to relieve his conscience, he instituted his award for the promotion of peace."[2]

Dynamite is a powerful thing. It can be used to bring people together, or it can be used to blow people apart. It can help make life better, or it can ruin someone's life altogether. It is a powerful tool that can give life and take it.

You and I were created by God with access to an internal, explosive power that can construct or destroy.

We all have a similar power within ourselves. We have access to something so strong—for good or for evil—that we bring life or death into situations on a regular basis. What's worrisome about this, though, is that most of us do not realize this power. And far too many of us let it ride roughshod over other people in our lives.

You and I were created by God with access to an internal, explosive power that can construct or destroy. It is the dynamite in our dentures—the tool known as the tongue.

The Muscle in Your Mouth

Your greatest enemy is not in your home. Your greatest enemy is not on your job. Your greatest enemy is not that person at church who gets on your every last nerve. Your greatest enemy is in your own mouth. That three-inch muscle in your mouth has more power to destroy your life, and to do it quickly, than anything or anyone else.

Your greatest enemy is in your own mouth.

If you grew up in a home similar to mine, your mom probably told you the same thing my mom told me: "Watch your mouth!" I would say something I probably shouldn't have said, and my mom would march right over to me with a stern look and say, "Boy, you'd better watch your mouth!" Then, depending on what it was, she might tell me to go wash my mouth out with soap!

Have you ever had to wash your mouth out with soap? It's disgusting—wiping that bar of soap on your tongue long enough to show your mom you actually did it. Your reflexes are making you gag, but you have to keep washing with the soap in order to get the job done. I know I didn't have to do that twice—once was enough for me to learn that lesson!

But watching your mouth is an important lesson to learn because the mouth has the power to destroy everything in its path. Someone once said, "The tongue is a wet place, and it can slip easily." You may be where you are today because someone spoke life into you. You may have had new roads and new opportunities created in your life because someone believed in you enough to speak words of life to you. Or you may be where you are right now because someone spoke things about you or to you that destroyed your dream, your hope, an expectation you had, or a relationship. Perhaps you have not yet recovered from the dynamite blasts you were hit with as a child. You could still be seeking to rebuild what was torn down because of what someone said to you.

The muscle in your mouth is no small thing. In fact, some couples have gotten divorced or are contemplating divorce because of the sticks of dynamite that continue to blow up their relationship. As a pastor who counsels church members on a weekly basis, I know that some people have not spoken to members of their family for years because the blast was so big and the pain was so deep, they have been unable to recover.

God might not use soap on our tongues to steer us in the right direction concerning this critical source of life or death in our mouths, but He does ask us to use some salt. "Your speech should always be gracious, seasoned with salt, so that you may know how you should answer each person," writes Paul (Colossians 4:6). Or if you don't prefer salt, He suggests some honey: "Pleasant words are a honeycomb: sweet to the taste and health to the body" (Proverbs 16:24).

Whether you are talking to a family member, a coworker, a clerk at the store, or even to yourself, your words carry the DNA of life or death.

God has a lot to say about our speech. In fact, the apostle James uses the first 12 verses of the third chapter of his epistle to give the most extensive statement in Scripture on the subject. Why does James devote so much time on such a matter? Because, as you will discover as we study what God's Word has to say concerning the power of your words, what you choose to say is no small thing. Whether you are talking to a family member, a coworker, a clerk at the store, or even to yourself, your words carry the DNA of life or death.

Since James covers this topic clearly in his epistle, I thought it best to begin this book by looking at the words that came out of his mouth. He begins with a warning: "Not many should become teachers, my brothers, knowing that we will receive a stricter judgment" (James 3:1). The first word out of the gate for James is a warning to people like myself and anyone else who seeks to disciple others according to the Word of God. I'm sure that includes you. Whether you are instructing your kids, helping a friend or family member, teaching a Sunday school class, or leading a small group, if you are yielding your life to the betterment of others, James gives you a strong warning to watch what you say—especially with regard to aligning your words underneath the comprehensive rule of God.

These days, social media makes it easy for people to offer their opinion on spiritual issues or things related to God's Word. I recently noticed that one very famous Christian singer who has been leading worship for decades—a name you would probably recognize if I mentioned it—posted on his Facebook page that he no longer believes the Bible is the Word of God. He said believers had turned it into an idol by placing too much value on it. I was shocked.

Not too long ago, people who spoke publicly about spiritual matters were often trained theologians or studied ministers who had devoted years to prayer and reading. But through the increased connectivity and communication we all have with each other through the Internet, opinions are now tossed around as if they were studied conclusions. Yet James warns of such things, saying that anyone who sets himself or herself up to give spiritual instruction to others, whether formally or informally, "will receive a stricter judgment."

We face a higher level of accountability anytime we
bring God and His name into the conversation.

A teacher speaks with the mouth. But even what is written or posted online is a product of the mouth. And James begins by reminding us that if we are going to express God's viewpoint on a matter, we had better pay careful attention to what that is. We face a higher level of accountability anytime we bring God and His name into the conversation.

After James's initial warning, he continues his lesson about our lips by establishing three unique points regarding the mouth, highlighting its power to direct life, to damage life, and to determine life.

Directing Life

James writes, "For we all stumble in many ways. If anyone does not stumble in what he says, he is a mature man who is also able to control his whole body" (James 3:2). He acknowledges that every person on the planet has made his or her share of mistakes. We have all stumbled in some way. But having made this broad statement, he goes on to instruct us regarding the person who does not stumble in what he says—that person, James tells us, is mature. People who can control what they say can also control the entire body.

If you will discover the secret of rightly ruling your mouth, you
will gain the ability to rightly rule your actions as well.

Yes, we all stumble in a variety of ways—in our relationships, in our finances, on the job—but James points out that if you can learn how to control what you say, that ability will then impact what you do. In essence, James says, "Give your lips to God, and He will give you your life." Or in other words, bridle your mouth, and the rest of you will follow.

Does anything seem to be going wrong in your life right now? If you will discover the secret of rightly ruling your mouth, you will gain the ability to rightly rule your actions as well.

Many believers today place a high value on church attendance, spiritual activity, prayers before meals, or any number of things. But James says there is one way to determine whether you are a mature believer—by noticing what comes out of your mouth. He writes, "If anyone thinks he is religious without controlling his tongue, then his religion is useless and he deceives himself" (James 1:26). According to this passage, many believers today are wasting their time doing a lot of religious activities while letting their loose lips make all manner of mess.

James gives us two illustrations to make his point. He begins by comparing the influence of our mouths to that of a bit and bridle in a horse's mouth. When Lois and I took our kids to family camp each summer at Pine Cove, we usually got to spend some time riding horses. If you've ridden a horse before, you know that you can control an entire 1500-pound beast of an animal with a little piece of metal placed just right in its mouth. If I wanted to make the horse go left, all I had to do was to move the reins so that the bit in his mouth would guide him in the direction I wanted to go. If I wanted to stop, I simply pulled back, and the bit in the horse's mouth brought him to a complete stop.

I don't mind riding a horse like that. But I wouldn't want to get on the back of a wild stallion, and I imagine you wouldn't either. A wild stallion that had never been brought under control would buck either of us right off.

─────────────────────

Your tongue is so powerful, it can literally steer the course of your life.

─────────────────────

Just as a person riding a horse uses a bit to control the entire body of the horse—even when the horse is much bigger and stronger—that three-inch muscle in your mouth can control your entire life. Your tongue is so powerful, it can literally steer the course of your life. An unbridled tongue—just like an unbridled horse—can cause serious damage to the rest of your life and to those in your path. Far too many people have ruined relationships and careers because of the explosions that have come out of their mouths.

Yet if you will learn to use the bit in your mouth—the dynamite in your dentures—for good, you will have the ability to steer your life, your relationships, and your work. You will also gain the ability to overcome the strongholds in your life you have been struggling to overcome. You will discover how to successfully navigate relationships in your home, at work, and in the church. You will have the power you need to direct your life choices toward the full, vibrant, and victorious life Christ came to give you.

But in order to do all that, you have to bring your tongue under control rather than letting it control you. You have to learn to watch your mouth.

James also compares the tongue to the rudder of a ship. We read, "And consider ships: Though very large and driven by fierce winds, they are guided by a very small rudder wherever the will of the pilot directs" (James 3:4).

---

*Your tongue may be small, but it will direct your
life. That is the way God designed it.*

The rudder of a ship is a small piece of equipment attached to an
enormous, heavy body of steel. Yet that small piece of equipment
determines the direction the boat will go. Your tongue may be small,
but it will direct your life. That is the way God designed it.

Damaging Life

If you don't learn to watch your mouth, you will set yourself up
for the next point James introduces in his discourse on the tongue.
You will experience the power in your mouth to do damage to your
life and the lives of those around you.

> So too, though the tongue is a small part of the body, it
> boasts great things. Consider how large a forest a small
> fire ignites. And the tongue is a fire. The tongue, a world
> of unrighteousness, is placed among the parts of our bod-
> ies. It pollutes the whole body, sets the course of life on
> fire, and is set on fire by hell.
>
> Every sea creature, reptile, bird, or animal is tamed
> and has been tamed by man, but no man can tame the
> tongue. It is a restless evil, full of deadly poison (James
> 3:5-8).

As I write this chapter, fires rage all the way from Alaska to Ari-
zona. More than 50 large wildfires have stripped the land, driving
thousands of people from their homes. These flames blaze to the tune
of billions of dollars of damage to property, yet they are often caused
by a single match. One match is not much to contend with, but if

you leave it alone long enough and don't address the damage it causes, you will face a fire too large to ignore. A fire that will consume in just a matter of minutes what took years to construct and establish. Very few things can withstand the heat of such a blaze.

What's worse is the time it takes to rebuild what was destroyed. Did you realize that it takes an average of eleven years for land to recover after it has been burned by a wildfire? And it takes decades for a forest to be reestablished. All because of a spark that turned into a flame and consumed the life that once was there.

Have you ever experienced anything like that in your own life? Not a literal forest fire, but a fire lit by your mouth—something you said? Maybe it was a wrong word at the wrong time. It could have been an inaccurate statement. It didn't have to be an entire paragraph to cause serious damage. One word can light another word, which lights another word…and before you know it, a marriage that seemed so strong and loving is now in divorce court. All it takes is one match to start a forest fire, and all it takes is a wrong word (or even an inappropriate tone of voice) to wreak havoc on a home.

On October 8, 1871, it only took one cow knocking over one lantern on the outskirts of old Chicago to start a fire that would burn for two days, claim more than 300 lives, destroy more than three miles of property, and leave more than 100,000 people homeless.

On April 28, 2015, it took only one word said the wrong way at one protest in Baltimore to get rocks flying, windows smashed, and flames burning down not only the local CVS Pharmacy but entire housing complexes.

One word. One sentence. One phrase can lead to a chain reaction of damage in property and in people's lives. For example, if the president of the United States says, "We're going to war," that's only one sentence. But that one sentence will cost lives, split families, and bring untold disaster. It's only a phrase, but it carries a lot of dynamite.

Hell is just waiting for a chance to influence our tongues.

Why can words do all of that? How can we start with one little disagreement and end up with family members refusing to speak to each other for years? Whether the rift is between coworkers, relatives, neighbors, or races, how can the mouth do so much damage?

James tells us how: "The tongue is a fire…and is set on fire by hell." The reason why your tongue and mine can do so much damage is that hell is just waiting for a chance to influence our tongues. When you or I speak, hell is looking for an opportunity to fan a spark into a fire. Satan purposefully and intently looks for ways to pour fuel on the fire of your speech so that what you say becomes bigger than you ever imagined.

Friend, your speech is not just your speech. Your speech can be empowered by hell.

James gives another illustration of the damage caused by the tongue when he talks of the beasts and birds, reptiles and sea creatures. He reminds us that all of these have been tamed by the human race, and yet no one can tame the tongue. Trainers have learned how to tame lions, entice tigers to jump through hoops, teach bears to ride bikes, or convince elephants to place a foot on someone's head without crushing them. All of this has been done with well-trained animals.

But how many times did your mother try to tame your tongue? How many times has your spouse reminded you that your tongue is not tamed—or vice versa? You may scold your children for not watching their mouth, but as soon as they enter their room and are out of earshot, they are likely to mumble something under their breath. This is because no man can tame the tongue.

Paul reminds us in his letter to the Romans that no one is without this sin: "There is no one righteous, not even one...Their throat is an open grave; they deceive with their tongues. Vipers' venom is under their lips. Their mouth is full of cursing and bitterness" (Romans 3:10,13-14).

Whoever controls your tongue controls your life.

Paul's point is clear—the tongue is unruly and refuses to be tamed. And remember, whoever controls the bit controls the beast. Whoever controls your tongue controls your life—your addictions, relationships, goals, and more.

Satan wants nothing more than to lull you into thinking that what comes out of your mouth does little damage at all. But in fact, your mouth (or someone else's) is the source of all damage and the catalyst for all the destruction you face.

Determining Life

After James discusses the power of your mouth to direct your life and to damage it, he dives into the power of the mouth to determine life.

> We praise our Lord and Father with it, and we curse men who are made in God's likeness with it. Praising and cursing come out of the same mouth. My brothers, these things should not be this way. Does a spring pour out sweet and bitter water from the same opening? Can a fig tree produce olives, my brothers, or a grapevine

produce figs? Neither can a saltwater spring yield fresh
water (James 3:9-12).

James reminds us that our mouths and our tongues can do something that even nature itself cannot do. We have the power to act in a
way that is outside the natural order of things. For example, you cannot go to a water fountain and out of that one opening get both fresh
and bitter water. You will either get fresh water or you will get bitter
water, but you won't get both out of the same place. Nor can you go
to a fig tree and get both apples and figs. You can only get figs from
of a fig tree. In nature, things produce only what they were designed
to produce. That's the way nature works.

But not the tongue. The tongue has the unique ability to contra-
dict itself. James tells us that we do this when out of the same mouth
come both blessing and cursing. One person can speak words that
create life and words that cause death. James tells us that this should
not be. Just as we don't want to be double-minded, we shouldn't be
double-tongued. We weren't designed to function that way. Rather,
we were created in the image and likeness of God. We bear the being
of God within us, and He is not like that.

When God created the world, He didn't roll up His sleeves and
get to work. Rather, God created the world and all that is in it with
His words. He spoke. God demonstrated the power of spoken words
when He said, "Let there be light," and there was light. The land
was separated from the water not because God started digging but
because God started talking. He used His mouth, not His hands.

When God described Jesus Christ, He
talked about speech—the Word.

Even more enlightening, when God introduced Jesus to us in John 1:1, He said, "In the beginning was the Word, and the Word was with God, and the Word was God." God went on to say in verse 14 that "the Word became flesh." When God described Jesus Christ, He talked about speech—the Word.

God's creative genius is in His speech. Even His own essence is in speech. When God chose to create something out of nothing, all He had to do was speak. When He wanted to teach Adam how to live his life, He gave Adam His word. Why? Because Adam was created in the image of God, so Adam was also given speech. The animals were not given speech—only humanity has this power. It is the power to give life and to take it. Proverbs 18:21 says, "Life and death are in the power of the tongue."

Our speech holds power beyond our wildest imaginations.

Just as God spoke the world and all life into being, you and I have the power to speak life or to speak death into our own lives and into each other. As beings created in the image of the one true God, we have been given a most powerful tool. Imagine how powerful speech must be if everything you see in the physical, tangible world was brought about through it. Now imagine what God wants to do in and through your mouth. He will use your words to bring you into your own personal destiny, and He will use your words to lead the people you influence into their destinies. Our speech holds power beyond our wildest imaginations.

Conversely, Satan brought death when he convinced Adam and Eve to believe his word.

A member of the church I pastor was decorated with several medals, including the Medal of Honor, after serving as a Marine in Vietnam. In one battle, eight of his men were wounded on the battlefield, and he alone went out to bring each person back to camp. Eight times he risked his own life in order to "leave no man behind."

Where did he find this courage?

The words of his father.

Shortly before he had left for war as a young man, his father took him aside to pray with him. Following that prayer, his father looked him in the eyes and said, "Son, I know you are coming back. I will see you again." His father had never lied to him before, so when he heard those words, he knew right then and there that he was going to make it back home alive. This belief gave him the courage to take risks on the battlefield that many men would not—all because of his father's words.

He not only made it back alive but also became a highly decorated veteran, honored and esteemed for his bravery on behalf of his comrades.

As individuals made in His image, our highest calling is to model with our mouths the image and character of God.

Words can save lives. Or from the same source, they can light a fire of destruction. The Lord tells us through James that this should not be. As individuals made in His image, our highest calling is to model with our mouths the image and character of God. We are His messengers.

Keep in mind that Satan knows this too. So he will try everything possible to trip you up in this one area of your life. Whoever controls the tongue, controls the future.

2

Lord of Your Lips

A ship was sailing at night when it received a radio message. The message was simple yet clear: "Turn south immediately. I am directly in front of you."

The captain of the ship did not want to turn south in the middle of the night or make any other change to his ship's course, so he replied, "I am a Navy captain. You turn north."

The captain waited briefly and then received another message. "You are headed straight toward me. Turn south now. I will not turn north."

The captain was irritated because this conversation was going on so long and also because the other person was not respecting his authority. So he replied, "This is my final statement. I am a Navy captain. I will not turn south. You will turn north."

He barely had time to send his message before he received an adamant reply. "You will turn south. I am a lighthouse."

Friend, regardless of who you are or what ship you are steering, the lighthouse will never adjust to you. It doesn't matter how powerful you are, how much education you have, or what successes you have had. If you are a ship in conflict with a lighthouse, the lighthouse will win every single time.

Unfortunately, many of us do not understand that. We believe we are setting our own courses and making our own decisions, and we expect everything else to adjust to us—including God. But if you and God are not seeing things the same way, you must adjust to Him. God will never adjust to you. If you want to call your own shots, go make your own world. This is God's world, and what He says goes.

Many of us like to dictate to God where we want Him to go and what we want Him to do, forgetting that He is the lighthouse and we are not. He directs the path, not us. He guides our way, not us. And He is Lord of our lips, not us. Chaos ensues when we set ourselves up as the ones who determine what we should say and when. When we do not surrender our thoughts and our words to God, we can expect negative outcomes as a result.

Words matter. What you say is no small thing. As we've seen already, life and death are in the power of the tongue. That is, with the tongue you can bless or curse, because your speech has spiritual repercussions.

As I began to compile my notes to teach and write on this topic of our words, I was interested to see how very little had been previously taught or written on the subject. That amazed me because there is precious little in our lives that carries such an enormous impact on our lives. Just as physical life and death are contained in the power of the heart, life and death—whether emotional, relational, spiritual, or even physical—are contained in the power of the tongue. We certainly would never downplay the role our heart has in our lives, and yet this subject of speech doesn't seem to get the airtime it deserves in Christian realms. Especially when it makes such a crucial contribution to our success or failure, individually and collectively.

Let's look at Matthew 16:21-23 to see just how difficult it can be to make our tongues work right.

> From then on Jesus began to point out to His disciples that He must go to Jerusalem and suffer many things from the elders, chief priests, and scribes, be killed, and be raised the third day. Then Peter took Him aside and began to rebuke Him, "Oh no, Lord! This will never happen to You!"
>
> But He turned and told Peter, "Get behind Me, Satan! You are an offense to Me because you're not thinking about God's concerns, but man's."

You can use the word "Lord" and yet be talking straight from the devil.

Those are three pregnant verses of Scripture. Peter begins by using what we would call "Christianese." He's using language that is familiar in Christian circles. He calls Christ "Lord," indicating that he is trying to think biblically, spiritually, and theologically. And yet despite his best attempts and seeking to shield and protect Jesus, when he finishes talking, Jesus refers to him as the devil. Evidently you can use the word "Lord" and yet be talking straight from the devil.

Now, what makes this very interesting is that a few verses earlier, Peter was hitting a bull's-eye. In verses 15-16 we find this conversation between Peter and Jesus: "[Jesus] asked them, 'Who do you say that I am?' Simon Peter answered, 'You are the Messiah, the Son of the living God!'" After that brief interchange, Jesus blessed Peter and called him a stone, establishing him as the leader for the birth of the church.

But a couple of verses later, Jesus rebukes Peter for speaking on behalf of Satan himself. That's how quickly the tongue can turn. Unless our heart, mind, and thoughts are aligned under God, there is no telling what will come out of our mouths. Only when Jesus is Lord of our lives will He also be Lord of our lips.

The word "Lord" means "master." To declare Jesus as Lord means that He is the One in control and is calling the shots in your life and your speech. To say "Lord" implies that He is the One controlling the discussion, your language, and your actions because He is the Master.

In fact, to call Jesus "Lord" is to call yourself a slave. This shows up in Romans, where Paul opens with these words: "Paul, a *slave* of Christ Jesus, called as an apostle and singled out for God's good news." Christ's half-brother James opens his book in a similar way: "James, a *slave* of God and of the Lord Jesus Christ." And Jude, also a half-brother of Jesus, writes, "Jude, a *slave* of Jesus Christ and a brother of James." Each of these leaders in the establishment of the Christian faith considered himself a slave.

The job of a slave is to follow the dictates of the master. As children of God, we are Christ's slaves. Yet too many of us want to be like Peter and simply use the word "Lord" while spouting our own opinions. We want Jesus as our Savior but don't want Him messing with us as Lord. When Jesus is your Lord, He is not your personal assistant. He's not your copilot. He is not your mentor.

Jesus Christ wants to own you. Jesus Christ *died* to own you.

Which means that you and I need to take a subservient position to His rule, surrendering to Him as Master over our thoughts, words, and life.

Before doubting Thomas came face-to-face with Jesus after His resurrection, he said he wouldn't believe unless he saw the holes in His hands and the hole in His side (John 20:25). When Jesus revealed

Himself to doubting Thomas, Thomas exclaimed, "My Lord and my God!" (verse 28). This is because he understood that to authentically call Him Lord meant He was also God.

The crisis we face today in Christianity is that very few believers are willing to become Christ's slaves. Very few Christians want to be owned by God. Yes, they want God to bless them. They want Him to heal them. They want Him to provide for them. But they do not want Him to own them. Most of us treat Jesus Christ the way the British treat the Queen of England. She's got a title; she just doesn't have any clout. Her subjects recognize and pay homage to her, but she doesn't get to pass any laws or make any decisions on national concerns.

Do you know what they give the Queen of England for her role? A weekly meeting. Once a week, she meets with the Prime Minister to get an update. Too often, we do the same with God. We come to church once a week to get our religious update, but we certainly won't let Jesus make any of our decisions. We aren't going to allow Him to control our lives or influence how we speak. Yes, we'll use His name up front, just as Peter did, but without God attached to it. We call Him Lord without surrendering to what that title really means.

I'm not saying we are evil because we try to take so much control of our language and what we say. Peter didn't mean any harm by trying to protect Jesus or by telling Him that everything was going to be okay. After all, he was just trying to help a brother out. He hears Jesus say that He's on His way to the cross to suffer and die, and Peter responds with a pushback. He puts up his hand and says, "Not on my watch, You're not!"

But that's precisely when Christ calls him the devil. Because that's precisely when Peter turned himself into his own god. He chose his own will and his own desires above God's, which is exactly what Lucifer did just before he got the boot out of heaven. You have the devil in your mouth anytime you speak that which stems from your desires or your perspectives rather than God's. That holds true even if those desires and perspectives aren't evil by our world's standards.

One thing you should never say is, "Jesus, I think You're wrong."

Whenever your desires disagree with what God wants, you are speaking outside of His will. It doesn't matter if you use His name, just as Peter did. People do that all the time these days. They put God's name on stuff that God has nothing to do with, and they don't say the things that align with Him. Peter didn't like what Jesus said, so he rejected it and argued instead. That's one argument you never want to have—an argument with God. You will lose every time. One thing you should never say is, "Jesus, I think You're wrong." That's not just you talking. That's the devil using you.

Get Behind Me

Peter used his mouth to join in on a view that was outside the will of God even though it was camouflaged by his use of the word "Lord." For Christ to be Lord of your lips, you have to give Him more than that one word. The entire sentence, paragraph, and point need to be surrendered and aligned to His will.

This explains why so many of our conversations go left so quickly. Two people start talking about something, and before they know it, an argument has ensued. It's because one or both parties let Satan have his way with their lips. And neither person was wise enough to say, "Get behind me, Satan." Jesus didn't hesitate when He noticed that the person He called a "stone" a few verses earlier—the future leader of the church—quickly turned into a stumbling block. He didn't sugarcoat His response or say, "I see that's how you feel, Peter. Thank you for sharing." Rather, Jesus rebuked Peter swiftly. He told him to get out of His way because Jesus had a mission to complete on behalf of the Father.

Do you realize that your tongue can actually block what God wants to do for you because your words are getting in His way? That's exactly the way Jesus described Peter's comment: "You are a stumbling block to Me; for you are not setting your mind on God's interests, but man's" (Matthew 16:23 NASB). In other words, Peter chose to think and react to a situation as an earthly minded person rather than a spiritually minded person, so he actually positioned himself between Christ and the Father's will. He became the roadblock as a result of his words.

Whenever you speak a word that disagrees with God's Word— even though you use God's name—Satan has poisoned your speech. Man's natural interests agree with Satan's interests. Any interest apart from God as Lord, Master, and Ruler is Satan's interest. When you come to realize how often our everyday conversations disagree with God's Word and His truth—through complaining, backbiting, pessimism, or the like—you will understand why your speech may be blocking your blessing.

When Peter agreed with God, Jesus told him he was blessed (Matthew 16:17). When he spoke out of sync with God's will, he became a mouthpiece for hell. Why? Because he revealed a heart that lacked faith in what God said to be true.

Your words are simply vocalizations of
your thoughts and your beliefs.

Your words are simply vocalizations of your thoughts and your beliefs. They reveal what you hold to be true. Since our blessing is often tied to our faith, when we speak words of fear, doubt, distrust, or the like, we are revealing a heart of fear, doubt, distrust, and so on. God rewards a heart of faith because without faith it is impossible to please Him (Hebrews 11:6). When God is not Lord of your lips, you position yourself to fall short of pleasing Him. View your speech through the lens of revelation—it reveals what you truly believe about the people you talk about, about the God you say you follow, and about yourself.

Take time to pay attention to what you say. Write it down if need be and count how many negative, untruthful statements you make in a day. They may be well-intentioned, just as Peter's were. But take note of what you say that disagrees with God. And each time you do, realize that you are standing in the way of God's plan for your life.

Remember when Satan tempted Eve to eat from the forbidden fruit in the garden? Even Satan sprinkled a little bit of God on top of what he said to get Eve to disobey. He introduced his temptation by saying, "Did God really say?" (Genesis 3:1). Satan knows how to talk smack. He can talk a good game any day of the week.

A man once came home from work to find his wife wearing a very expensive outfit she had just purchased. She asked how she looked, and he asked how much it cost. When she told him the price, he almost hit the ceiling, so the first thing he said was, "How on earth could you spend so much money on that dress?"

The wife replied, "Well, I tried it on, and the devil told me I looked stunning."

"So why didn't you tell the devil to get behind you when he said that?" the husband replied.

"I did," the wife said, "and the devil said I looked even better from back there!"

The devil knows what to say to get you out of alignment with God's will. He can talk sweet, soft, and subtle. And as we just saw with Eve in the garden, he doesn't mind tossing God's name in there too. It's not whether God's name is mentioned that ultimately makes Jesus Lord of our lips; it's whether what we say is aligned with His comprehensive rule over every area of our lives.

When you come to understand that your words have the power to invite either God or Satan into a conversation, you will want to watch your mouth. Satan loves to create a conflict of interests between our will and God's will. And our will is far stronger than you realize. In fact, if you start to watch your mouth seriously, your soul is going to throw a temper tantrum. Just as small children may whine when they don't like what you tell them to do, your soul will grumble and complain when it has to align your thoughts and words with God's will rather than its own.

If you aren't accustomed to letting God be the Lord of your lips, and if you have decided to submit yourself to His lordship over your mind so that He can control your mouth, your soul is going to have to make a major adjustment. This is because your soul is used to telling you what to do. It is not used to God telling you what to do. This is a perfect illustration of the principle Christ introduces in verse 24, just after rebuking Peter. He says, "If anyone wants to come with Me, he must deny himself, take up his cross, and follow Me." To make Christ Lord of your lips, you will have to deny your soul's desire to have its own way in what you say.

One of Satan's primary objectives is to control your soul so that he can keep you distant from God. And when it doesn't work one way, he'll try another. Satan never gets weary of going on the offense. We see him hitting hard on Peter in a different situation when Jesus tells Peter that Satan had asked to sift the disciples like wheat (Luke 22:31-34).

Peter spoke up again in this situation and assured Christ that he would never falter: "Lord, I'm ready to go with You both to prison and to death!" (verse 33).

We all know how that story turned out.

Three rooster crows later, and it's a curtain call on Peter. It's a wrap. He can punch his time card and go home. Why? Because pride goes before a fall. Peter thought he was so strong that Satan could not mess with him. But once you get to that place, you've lost. Why? Because God hates pride. To be prideful is to consider yourself to be more high and mighty than you are.

When God sees your pride, He backs away from you. When God hears your praise to Him on Sunday but notices you don't seem to need Him on Monday, He backs off. He says, "Go ahead and run your own life. Make your own plans. Do your own thing."

No one is too strong for Satan to attack—except God Himself. You are not. I am not. Yet when we live and speak as if we were, we wind up being dominated by our decisions and controlled by our circumstances. We also talk to God with the lips of Lucifer. Remember, it was Lucifer's lips that planted a kiss from Judas on Jesus's cheek. To let a fool kiss you is stupid, but to let a kiss fool you is worse. You have to be wise, otherwise God replies, "I can't bless that." He can't when we insist on using our own minds and mouths in our own power.

If the Lord Wills

In the book of James we find one of the most potent passages on the tongue and God's view of how we often use it.

> Come now, you who say, "Today or tomorrow we will go to such and such a city, and spend a year there and engage in business and make a profit." Yet you do not know what your life will be like tomorrow. You are just a vapor that appears for a little while and then vanishes away. Instead,

you ought to say, "If the Lord wills, we will live and also
do this or that." But as it is, you boast in your arrogance;
all such boasting is evil (James 4:13-16 NASB).

I can imagine God leaning up against a wall, crossing His arms,
and looking down at us with all our fancy business ideas and plans
for what we are going to accomplish in the next year or the next five
years, all the while shaking His head. After all, we are boasting about
something over which we have absolutely no control. When we do
that, we are bragging about our plans independently of God. Only
God is to say whether any of us will even be here next year.

Beyond that, God will sometimes take us down a different path
or on a different journey than we could have conceived or imagined.
The simple phrase we are asked to insert, "If the Lord wills," is pregnant with meaning. It is a statement of surrender under the lordship
and rule of God. It is an acknowledgment that our plans are not to be
our own. Rather, they are God's to make, and we are to follow.

One of our greatest tragedies is that we sometimes plan God right
out of our lives. We don't give Him room to interrupt. This happens
when we follow the path we feel is best rather than the path He leads
us on. Or when our schedules are so tight that we have no room for
surrender.

When you don't leave room for God to interrupt your plans, you
set yourself up to be sorely disappointed because He definitely will
interrupt. God has a way of intervening when He desires. There is no
such thing as planning independently of God because He is the One
who controls the outcome. And since God is the One controlling the
outcome, it is unwise to make plans apart from Him. After all, God
has a way of turning detours into a lifestyle until He gets you to the
place He was preparing for you to be.

Punctuate your sentences with the phrase "If the Lord wills"
from now on and let it be a guiding truth in your spirit and in your

thoughts. Hold your plans with an open hand. Gripping them tight will only cause you pain when God reaches in to make changes.

None of us are promised a tomorrow, so we should make our plans with God and eternity in mind. Otherwise, when we boast about what we will be doing, we invite Satan into the conversation. We invite pride, which leads to a fall.

In Luke 12:13-21, Jesus told a story about rich man whose plan for retirement included building bigger barns and storing all his treasures there. But before he could even implement his plan, God showed up and said, "You fool! This very night your soul is demanded of you. And the things you have prepared—whose will they be?" (Luke 12:20). When you leave God out of the contingencies of life, His will trumps your own.

If the Lord wills.

If He can steer your speech, He can steer your life—for His glory and your good.

Why? Because He is the boss and we are the slaves. At the end of the day, that's what it comes down to. God is in charge. God is in control. And He wants to be Lord of your lips. When God gets hold of your tongue, He has the rest of you too. If He can steer your speech, He can steer your life—for His glory and your good.

Making It Public

God wants you to do more than believe what He says and think on it. He also wants you to speak what He says. He is in charge and is ultimately in control, so let His words *to* you become your words *from* you.

In Matthew 10:27 (NASB) we read, "What I tell you in the darkness, speak in the light; and what you hear whispered in your ear, proclaim upon the housetops." It's amazing what we will spend our time talking about these days—television shows, celebrities, our coworkers...we'll talk openly about all these things even when salacious and immoral behavior is involved. But when it comes to the things of God, many of us choose to put our finger to our lips and hush. We are keeping quiet about the wrong thing! Why are we silent about God but vocal about everything else?

Wrong speaking will come back to bite you,
but right speaking will reward you.

The Lord tells us to speak what we hear in the secret place. Church is one secret place—a safe environment where everyone pretty much agrees with everyone else. God tells us that when we go out into the world—into the society—where people are cussing, fussing, and conniving, He wants us to talk about what we learned in church. What we learned in His Word. What His viewpoint of a matter is. That is to be the purpose of what we say. God is to be Lord of our lips. He made them, so let Him use them for His intention, good, and glory.

Friend, wrong speaking will come back to bite you, but right speaking will reward you. Look at what Christ says: "Therefore everyone who confesses Me before men, I will also confess him before My Father who is in heaven" (Matthew 10:32 NASB). Confess Christ publicly, and you get a mention before the King of the universe. To confess is to say the same thing—to speak the same sentiment and truth that God would be saying. It is to be on the same page as God. Jesus says that if you are not willing to do that before men, He will not do the same for you before God. Why should He?

God does not want to be hidden in your conversation. God does not want us to be ashamed when His name is mentioned. You and I are exposed to lewd language every day, thanks to the entertainment industry. In everyday conversations, people speak coarsely without apology. But how many of us are boldly speaking the thoughts, perspective, and words of God? God's perspective usually differs from the world's. As Christians, we are to speak the truth *in love*, but we are still to speak the truth. We aren't to shrug our shoulders and say, "Um..."

Our conversations matter to God. What we post on social media matters to God. What we say matters to God because life and death are in the power of our tongues.

Agree with God in what you say, and you will
see Him make a way out of no way.

That's why Romans 10:9-10 (NASB) says, "If you confess with your mouth Jesus as Lord, and believe in your heart that God raised Him from the dead, you will be saved; for with the heart a person believes, resulting in righteousness, and with the mouth he confesses, resulting in salvation." The Greek word translated "salvation" in this verse means "deliverance." The deliverance you desire and have sought all these years comes from your own mouth and what you choose to do with it. Agree with God in what you say, and you will see Him make a way out of no way. Bring God into the equation, and He will control the environment.

Jesus is powerful, and the words He speaks are powerful as well (John 6:63). So when you speak His Word, you are accessing and utilizing His power. That's why we are instructed to let His words live large inside us (Colossians 3:16).

Let Christ be Lord over your lips, and He will be Lord over your life—giving you full access to His wisdom, grace, power, victory, and freedom. That seems like a pretty good trade, wouldn't you say?

3

God in Your Gums

We have all been to the zoo. Either we have gone ourselves with a friend, taken our children or grandchildren, or been taken as children way back when.

In every zoo you will find that the most vicious animals are in cages simply because they are so dangerous. The cages have bars or a solid glass wall to keep the animal inside. The cage is the container, limiting how far the lion, tiger, or gorilla can go. We know that if those dangerous animals ever broke out of their cages, someone would get hurt.

From time to time, even at the most prepared and well-kept zoos, this has happened. A person accidentally leaves a feeding door open, or an animal somehow leaps over the container wall. When that has occurred, the results for those nearby have been devastating or even deadly.

This incarceration is necessary in order to keep these dangerous animals from doing serious damage.

God knew that the tongue was so dangerous, He put it behind

bars—our teeth. Then He stuck it in a cage—our mouth. God knew that if ever the tongue were to be let loose, it had the capacity and instinct to do a considerable amount of damage. In fact, it could even prove deadly to a situation or relationship (Proverbs 16:28).

The tongue contains so much damaging potential that I'm surprised to find so little teaching on it in our churches, in our books, or in one-on-one discipleship. The tongue can slice and dice someone or ruin a relationship in an instant. Most people have lamented, "I wish I hadn't said that," or "I wish that had not been said to me, and in that way." In fact, the number one reason for relational discord and divorce has to do with the tongue—communication. Over and over again, couples tell me in counseling sessions, "We just don't know how to communicate."

If you can learn how to shape your speech, you will have discovered the power to shape your life.

If you can learn how to shape your speech, you will have discovered the power to shape your life. But the question remains, how do you shape your speech so that it works for you rather than against you? In a passage found in Exodus, chapter 4, we can gain some insights into answering that question. The events occurred when Moses had been tending sheep in the desert for nearly 40 years.

Moses had been raised in the lap of luxury as an adopted child of Pharaoh's daughter. As a result, he had also received the best training available to mankind at that time. Confidence, charisma, and charm belonged to this young, powerful future ruler. His words and his actions held power (Acts 7:22). Moses wanted to free his people (the Israelites) from his adopted people (the Egyptians), but he moved too quickly, and as a result, he made enemies on both sides.

Chased into the middle of nowhere by his legitimate fears of retaliation, Moses wound up trading the elegance of Egypt for the dust of the desert. He found himself tending sheep instead of leading people. And after four decades of what was most likely boredom, frustration, and struggle, Moses had lost his mojo. He had lost his belief in himself. He had lost his hope.

Upon meeting the Creator in the burning bush and hearing of an assignment well beyond what he now felt he could accomplish, Moses responded with these words: "Please, Lord, I have never been eloquent—either in the past or recently or since You have been speaking to Your servant—because I am slow and hesitant in speech" (Exodus 4:10).

Moses's own view of himself had slid so far from what it once was that he even claimed he had never been able to speak well. It could be that the assignment of going back to Pharaoh at this time in his life and telling Pharaoh to let God's people go intimidated him so much that he looked for an excuse. Whatever the case, God did not accept Moses's reply. Rather, He said, "Who made the human mouth? Who makes him mute or deaf, seeing or blind? Is it not I, Yahweh? Now go! I will help you speak and I will teach you what to say" (verses 11-12).

Moses's fear of approaching Pharaoh seems reasonable. After all, most of us probably have some form of trepidation when speaking with someone who is powerful or in authority, especially when they don't necessarily want to hear what we have to say.

Have you ever gotten a traffic ticket? If you showed up on the court date to stand before the judge, who held your fate in her hands, did you notice a slight quiver in your voice when you answered her questions? That's normal. Something about authority and power intimidates most of us. In fact, most people just skip the appearance altogether and pay the fine. Why put yourself in that position?

Moses was seeking to do the same. God had asked him to appear before a powerful leader and make an incredulous request. Of course he stumbled over his words in his reply to Almighty God and tried to back out of the mission. This was a "mission impossible" he did not want to accept. Moses didn't want to talk to Pharaoh. He didn't feel prepared to make this plea. And that's why God had to give him a lesson in theology.

> Who made the human mouth?
> Who makes him mute or deaf, seeing or blind?
> Is it not I, Yahweh?
> Now go!
> I will help you...
> I will teach you what to say.

God asked Moses a rhetorical question—who created his mouth, anyhow? Did God make a mistake when He made Moses's mouth? No. Regardless of Moses's insecurities and frailties, God was fully aware and fully in charge.

God told Moses to do something with that which He Himself made (Moses's mouth), but Moses told God he could not do it. That means Moses was putting himself in a position of trumping God. Essentially, Moses was saying, "I'm the one calling the shots, and I'm not going."

But God made Moses's mouth, so He wasn't about to accept that response. After all, He would be with Moses and teach him what to say at the right time and in the right way. Did you know that a major part of God's relationship with you involves Him being Lord over your lips? Just as God was with Moses, so He is with you. You need not fear that you won't know the right thing to say in an intimidating situation, because when you discover how to rely on the power of the Holy Spirit, He will give you the words to say. He will dictate to you while you speak and carve out your conversation.

You may feel nervous about talking with a particular person or dealing with a difficult situation, but this lesson from the life of Moses reminds each of us that God is able to guide our speech when we let Him. He told Moses what to say, and He will do the same for you and me.

In our contemporary culture, politicians have speech writers. Speech writers are uniquely skilled to craft the cadence of speech, and they know which points to emphasize and which delicate issues to de-emphasize. Speech writers know how to calm people and how to rouse them to action, how to win people over and how to inspire them to support the politician's mission or goal. The speech writer considers the politician's topic and audience and then carves out the content, making it palatable to the hearers.

The God of the universe is offering to be your speech writer.

Friend, God is saying to you and me as He did to Moses, "I want to be your speech writer—and I'm the best speech writer around!" The God of the universe is offering to be your speech writer, and who knows the nuances of your life, work, and relationships better than God? Who knows how to address them better than He does?

This is a big deal because words are a big deal to God. Whenever God wanted to create something, He spoke it into existence. He said, "Let there be light," and there was light. He used words not merely to convey content, but to achieve His purpose and to create something new. God doesn't speak simply because He is in a talkative mood, as so many of us do. His words work out His will.

How incredible is that? The God who made your mouth will also fill it. He *wants* to fill it. We read, "I am Yahweh your God, who brought you up from the land of Egypt. Open your mouth wide, and I will fill it" (Psalm 81:10). God will communicate *to* you so He can communicate *through* you and accomplish something *beyond* you.

Wasted Words

Have you ever been in a conversation that left you feeling as if nothing was accomplished? Have you ever felt that the words were wasted? That happens a lot more than we realize, but that never happens with God's words. That's why He wants to be your speech writer—His words will never be wasted. His words always bring about His intended result (Isaiah 55:11).

Yet this raises some questions. How do you give God the job? How do you allow Him to be your speech writer and control your content? How do you have God maneuver in your mouth so that you are saying precisely the right word for precisely the right moment?

Jesus gives us the answer to those questions and more in John 12:49: "I have not spoken on My own, but the Father Himself who sent Me has given Me a command as to what I should say and what I should speak." Every word that the Son of God said was perfect, it was well timed, and it accomplished the intended outcome. This is because when He talked, He spoke only the words God told Him to say. He had such an abiding and submissive relationship with the Father that God's words became His own.

When Christ died and rose from the dead, you and I each received the power to have the fullness of that same abiding intimacy with the Father through the gift of the Holy Spirit. And one of the Holy

Spirit's primary roles is to speak on God's behalf (John 16:13-14). This theme shows up in Scripture on a number of occasions, such as Mark 13:11: "When they arrest you and hand you over, don't worry beforehand what you will say. On the contrary, whatever is given to you in that hour—say it. For it isn't you speaking, but the Holy Spirit." The Holy Spirit is so positioned in our lives that He is able to speak through us. If we learn to abide in Him, we don't need to worry about what to say. The Holy Spirit will tell us what we ought to say. He will give us the words of God for our particular situation, conversation, or relationship.

Yet if you don't know how to hear and discern the Holy Spirit speaking *to* you, He won't be able to speak *through* you. That is why time with God—an abiding presence with Him—is so critical to living out your destiny and fulfilling all God has for you. The Holy Spirit is often compared to a dove. Now, doves don't roar like lions. You have to listen for the coo. In the Old Testament, we read of God speaking in a whisper and not in the wind or earthquake or fire (1 Kings 19:11-13). Although we would probably appreciate Him doing it from time to time, the Holy Spirit does not grab a bullhorn when He has something to say to us. He leads us in love, not in domination. He honors our free will and lets us choose whether to move forward, to stagnate, or even to backtrack.

Hearing the Holy Spirit and allowing Him to speak through you is critical if you are to use your mouth to multiply the good and God's blessing in your life. With the Holy Spirit, you receive the specific guidance you need for a specific moment in time.

For example, people who know me well know I'm a news connoisseur. I like to listen to all things news, but mostly I prefer to listen to national news. However, I don't turn on the national news if I want to hear about the local weather or the traffic on a nearby route. I have to go to the local news for that information. The national news provides the overall picture of the world and the nation, and the local news gives me what I need to know about the area where I live.

The Holy Spirit tells you how to apply scriptural truths to your personal situation.

Similarly, Scripture gives each of us the overarching truths and principles for life. Yet Scripture does not tell you what to say to your boss when he is disappointed with an assignment you turned in. Nor does it tell you what to say to your spouse who is having a particularly grumpy week. It doesn't tell you what to say to a friend who just experienced a devastating loss. That's the Holy Spirit's job.

The Holy Spirit tells you how to apply scriptural truths to your personal situation. The Holy Spirit lets you know what you need to say to move forward, resolve conflict, diffuse emotions, achieve success, and more. Yet unless you learn how to walk in the Spirit and hear His voice speaking to your mind so He can dictate to your mouth, you will miss out on how He wants to specifically lead you to address your situation.

Who Is Calling the Plays?

The National Football League has a rule book that governs all 32 teams. The book gives them the rules of the game, and all the rules apply to every team. However, every team has its own playbook. The playbook is different from the rule book because the playbook is unique to each team, its scheme, and its personnel. This playbook outlines specific plays to call in specific situations. Now of course, the playbook has to be aligned under the rule book, but the playbook carries its own instructions within those parameters.

In life, the rule book is God's standard for everyone—don't gossip or slander, speak what is kind, and more. But the playbook is the approach within that standard for your particular life. The Holy Spirit has your playbook and is willing to give you everything you need to be successful on the field of life. That's why it is critical to stay so close to the Holy Spirit that you can hear Him even when He gives last-second directions.

In football, each play is called in the huddle. But when the team lines up and the quarterback sees the defense, he may call an audible, changing the play on the spot. He yells out a code word to his team to let them know they need to forget what they just discussed in the huddle and listen closely to him right then. If a player chooses to ignore the quarterback's audible and instead goes with the play called in the huddle…well, he's not likely to be playing much football after that. One key to success in football is the ability to listen and adjust when a new play is called. Likewise, one key to success in life is the ability to listen and adjust when the Holy Spirit provides fresh guidance and direction.

The Holy Spirit wants to call audibles in your communication, but if you aren't in contact with Him, you won't hear Him. You'll be going with an old play for a new situation. When that happens, everything is off. That's why husbands and wives could be talking about scrambled eggs and an hour later talking about getting a divorce. There was a shift along the way, and one or both did not discern how to adjust. Someone moved. The conversation changed. What started as a conversation ended up as a fight over something that had nothing to do with the original conversation at all. All because they were not hearing from heaven.

God wants to be your speech writer, but in addition to that, He wants to be able to edit your words on the spot. Have you ever typed out an email, adjusted each phrase to make it just right, read through the entire message one last time…and then deleted it and started all over? God wants to edit your words as you say them, giving you the ability to make changes and respond to whatever situation you are facing. Satan isn't sitting still when it comes to stirring up conflict all around us. The way to defeat him is through the Holy Spirit's freedom to respond through us to whatever Satan throws our way.

Having the Holy Spirit will do little unless you engage the Spirit and allow Him to lead you.

A car is simply a metallic body pieced together. Without an engine, it is unable to go anywhere at all. The Holy Spirit is the engine within you that empowers you to accomplish all God has intended for you to do. Yet simply having an engine in a car isn't enough—you must turn the key and engage it. Having the Holy Spirit will do little as well unless you engage the Spirit and allow Him to lead you. So how do you engage the Holy Spirit in your life in order to lead you? It's as easy as turning on your car. You simply ask Him.

> So I say to you, keep asking, and it will be given to you. Keep searching, and you will find. Keep knocking, and the door will be opened to you. For everyone who asks receives, and the one who searches finds, and to the one who knocks, the door will be opened. What father among you, if his son asks for a fish, will give him a snake instead

of a fish? Or if he asks for an egg, will give him a scorpion?
If you then, who are evil, know how to give good gifts to
your children, how much more will the heavenly Father
give the Holy Spirit to those who ask Him? (Luke 11:9-13).

It's a familiar passage with an often overlooked key. The method
to engaging the Holy Spirit actively in your life is to ask Him. Just ask.
Whatever you need and whenever you need it, ask the Father for the
Spirit's guidance, and He will respond to your request. I love the way
Isaiah 50:4 puts it: "The Lord God has given Me the tongue of those
who are instructed to know how to sustain the weary with a word."
Isaiah says outright that his tongue is instructed. His tongue has been
taught to say the right thing.

Speaking rightly doesn't come naturally to anyone born with a sin
nature. Yet when you yield your lips to the Lord, the Spirit will put
His ideas in your mind and make them audible through your mouth.
This is what Scripture calls being filled with the Holy Spirit.

The Bible also compares this process to drinking wine. "Don't get
drunk with wine, which leads to reckless actions, but be filled by the
Spirit" (Ephesians 5:18). If you have ever been drunk or witnessed
someone who was drunk, you know that the alcohol influences the
mind in such a way that people no longer speak or act as themselves.
Many a relationship and a life have been ruined by alcohol due to its
mind-altering effects.

God uses this illustration to help us understand how we are to be
impacted by the Holy Spirit. We are to be so yielded to the Spirit that
He dominates what we say, how we talk, how we walk, and what we
do. When the Holy Spirit governs your speech, others will recognize
that the words aren't coming from you alone. They will notice that
you are not responding in a typical manner—with anger, knee-jerk
reactions, accusations, blame, self-pity, criticism, and the like.

So how do you get filled with the Spirit? The same way you get drunk with wine—you consume it. You abide in the Spirit's presence and open your heart to His own. In humility, you acknowledge His divine wisdom and direction and ask Him to make this known to you throughout your day and at night. Rather than resisting, as Moses initially did at the burning bush, you follow Isaiah's example and say, "Lord, here am I. Send me." You trust that the Holy Spirit will give you the words to say in each and every situation God appoints for you.

When you live your life with God in your gums, allowing Him to be Lord over your lips, He will tell you where to go, what to do, and what to say. Just as a tiny rudder can direct an entire ship, God will use your tongue to do amazing things, even beyond your wildest expectations.

Once Moses yielded himself, God used his messed-up mouth to free an entire nation from hundreds of years of slavery. I'd say that was beyond anyone's expectations.

God can do great things through you too.

4

Power in Your Palate

Are you facing a major issue in your life right now? I'm referring not to the minor things you can cope with easily, but rather to a serious situation that looms larger than life. Scripture sometimes calls these trials and challenges "mountains." When the Bible speaks symbolically of a mountain—not a physical location but rather a spiritual issue—it is talking about something too big for you to climb, too wide for you to go around, and too thick to pass through. A mountain represents an oversized situation that is limiting your progress and blocking you from moving forward.

Mountains can come in all shapes and sizes. Sometimes they rise up because of our own poor choices, but often they appear through no fault of our own.

Sometimes people are mountains. Perhaps it is the person you work with—your boss, your coworker, or someone you supervise. You have to see this person five days a week, and you can't do anything to change that. Or it could be a family member, a friend, a neighbor…you name it.

Maybe you are under a mountain of debt. Perhaps your health issues are like a mountain. Whatever your mountain is, you just can't seem to get over it. It's too big.

Such is the symbolism we find in Mark 11:20-23, which sets the scene for our next lesson on the power of the mouth.

> Early in the morning, as they were passing by, they saw the fig tree withered from the roots up. Then Peter remembered and said to Him, "Rabbi, look! The fig tree that You cursed is withered."
>
> Jesus replied to them, "Have faith in God. I assure you: If anyone says to this mountain, 'Be lifted up and thrown into the sea,' and does not doubt in his heart, but believes that what he says will happen, it will be done for him."

Jesus and His disciples had passed by the fig tree the previous day, but they had found nothing on it but leaves. Jesus had been hungry and was obviously disappointed to find a fig tree without figs (even though it was not the season for figs), so He had said, "May no one ever eat fruit from you again" (verse 14). His words didn't accompany any special song, dance, or movement. He didn't wave a wand or rip up the roots. Jesus simply made one statement to the tree and then walked away. I would imagine the disciples thought very little of it at the time.

Later that day, Jesus went to the temple with His disciples. What He saw there made Him angry—money changers turning the temple complex into a marketplace and taking advantage of out-of-town worshippers. He overturned their tables and drove them out. Jesus was essentially reflecting the same sentiment to the merchants that He did to the tree. Like the tree, they gave false promises. They appeared to have life but actually had none at all.

The next day, Jesus and His disciples were returning from the temple and happened to pass by the same tree. When they did, it caught Peter's attention. Why? Because the tree had looked healthy and full of leaves the day before, but in that short amount of time, it had withered from the bottom to the top. It had completely decayed. Peter pointed this out to Jesus because trees don't typically wither in a day.

Faith, coupled with our own words, is what Jesus wants us to use in our lives to bring about miracles.

Jesus took advantage of this teachable moment with Peter to share with him (and ultimately with us) that what happened to the tree wasn't simply about the tree. Rather, it was a demonstration of the power of belief combined with the spoken word. Christ's belief and His words caused that tree to wither so quickly. This same faith, coupled with our own words, is what Jesus wants us to use in our lives to bring about miracles.

I use the word "miracle" because that's what it takes to move a mountain. I'm not talking about simply finding a prime parking spot at a crowded grocery store or an airport. I'm talking about those things in your life that cannot be reversed or resolved without a miracle. Remember, a mountain is so big that you can't climb over it, you can't go around it, you can't go through it…it's a beast.

Jesus tells us the way you conquer this beast is by speaking to it. In this illustration, He doesn't even tell us to speak to God about the situation. Rather, we are to speak directly to the situation itself. Jesus says we are to speak in faith to the mountain.

Which is exactly what He had done to the tree. He had been hungry but had found no figs on the tree, so He had walked over to it and said, "May no one ever eat fruit from you again." Jesus spoke directly to an inanimate object. And what's more, the inanimate object responded to His words.

The next day, when Jesus instructed His disciples about faith, He assured them that the approach He used with the tree also applied to anything in their own lives—even mountains.

In familiar Bible stories like this one, it's easy to skim over Christ's words. But let's pause for a moment and look carefully at what He said, because the words He chose are revealing. He said, "If anyone says *to this* mountain, 'Be lifted up and thrown into the sea,' and does not doubt in his heart, but believes that *what he says* will happen, *it will be done* for him." I've italicized the parts I want you to look at closely.

Let's also review what Jesus did not say. Jesus did not say that to move a mountain, we need to bow our heads, confess our sins, sing our songs, and then pray a long, eloquent prayer to God. All of those things are good, they're important, and they have their place because God is to be the subject of our faith. But Jesus did not say they were essential to moving any mountains. What Jesus said to His disciples (and ultimately to you and me) is that we are to speak to the mountain and tell it to move without doubting in our hearts—and it will move.

Period.

Friend, there *is* power in your palate.

There are two extremes in evangelical circles when it comes to this matter of speaking to the mountains in our lives. On one hand, many evangelicals emphasize studying Scripture, learning what it says, memorizing it…but they don't teach us how to actually *speak* it. As a result, we find believers who are biblically literate but who are powerless when it comes to dealing with the adverse circumstances (the mountains) in their lives.

On the other hand, many other evangelicals so emphasize speaking to their mountains (often referred to as speaking things into existence) that they teach things that are inconsistent with God's Word, leaving them equally powerless.

So let me be clear. How can you be sure that the words you are speaking to your mountain are the words God wants you to say? How can you be confident that your faith is in God and not in your own words? Here is the key: Your words must be aligned with Scripture.

Saying whatever you want won't move mountains. And merely knowing what Scripture says won't move mountains. But you *can* overcome the big challenges in your life by speaking the truths of Scripture directly to your situation.

Authorized Power

Let's look at the order of what Jesus said to His disciples to gain insight into how to use our words for good. He begins by telling them, "Have faith in God." Before they say anything to the mountain at all, they are to have faith. This is because what they believe will determine what they say as well as the impact of their words. The same is true for you and me. Before we say anything, we must believe something to be true. Only then will our words have transformational impact.

For example, when God created the world and said such things as "Let there be light," those words would not have carried any weight without His ability to bring them to fruition. In other words, God brings things about in reality by what He says. Before you see it, God said it. And before God said it, He thought it. Words are thoughts made audible. God thought it, He said it, and it was done.

God doesn't have to check with Himself to see whether He will bring something about. He gets to skip that part. But since you and I are not God, we must begin with this truth: Have faith in God. Once our heart's desire aligns with His perspective, whatever we say in faith can and will come about. This principle is replete in Scripture.

Your declaration must first have His authorization.

Our words carry no weight if they are not rooted in faith in God's will and power. For example, if you were to go to work tomorrow and your coworker said to you, "You're fired," you probably wouldn't get too nervous. But if your boss said the same thing, that's a different story. When people are authorized to speak, their words carry weight. The authorization is what matters. So before you try to move any mountains, align your faith under God's rule and perspective. Your declaration must first have His authorization.

Let me put it this way. We all have power in our homes because we are connected to a source of electricity. When you pay your bills on time, the power company authorizes you to use their power. However, the power company is not going to come to your house and plug in your television or appliances. You have to do that. All they do is authorize you to use the power.

Two things must happen for your appliances to work. First, you must connect them to the authorized power. Second, you must turn them on. If you fail to do either of those two things, you will not access the power you need. Likewise, to move mountains, two things must occur. You must have faith in God's authorized power, and you must turn on that power with your words. In this way, you connect the invisible realm with the visible world. You bring heaven into history.

Now, there's a trick to this that many of us miss, and it's found in Mark 11:24. "Therefore I tell you, all the things you pray and ask for—believe that you have received them, and you will have them." Did you catch that? Jesus uses two different tenses in the same sentence. He says, "believe that you have received them [present perfect tense], and you will have them [future tense]."

Sometimes we pray that we will have something in the future or that God will do something in the future, and that's fine. But sometimes God wants us to pray that we already have something or that it is already done. By praying that you already have it while simultaneously believing that it is done, you are praying in full faith. You are releasing what God has already intended to do (Isaiah 65:24). Prayer doesn't get God to do what He doesn't want to do. Prayer releases what God has already intended. Faith acknowledges that truth.

When we pray, we aren't using our words to coax God or to motivate Him. He has already determined what He is going to do. Rather, when we pray or believe something in faith, we are plugging our personal situations (our appliances) into God's power (the utility company). That's why you and I can (and should) often pray in the present perfect tense—that we already have what we're asking for. That's why you and I can (and should) believe that things have already been handled. God is not bound by time and space as we know it.

Think about it. If someone has already decided to do something and accomplished it, you don't have to push them to do it. All you have to do is thank them for it. Words that contain authentic faith simply affirm that something has already been done in the spiritual realm, and they bring it into your experiential reality.

One of the greatest tragedies in the church today is that much of the preaching is often left in the pew. Much of the Bible is often left between the front and back cover. If the Word of God does not proceed from our thoughts to our mouths in faith, it remains dormant and useless. We use it when we say it. God's Word must be more than just heard. It must be believed and spoken. This is because it is not simply speech. Rather, it is God's authoritative revelation, which contains the power to move mountains.

When God's Word proceeds out of our mouths, we tap into a power source that is beyond us.

Satan tempted Jesus in the desert at a vulnerable time in His life. Jesus was isolated from His friends, and He was weak and hungry from fasting. Jesus responded to the devil's temptations by having a Bible study with him. When the devil tempted Him to turn stones to bread, Christ replied, "Man must not live on bread alone but on every word that comes from the mouth of God" (Matthew 4:4). It is the Word of God—from His mouth—that provides the sustenance and power of life. When God's Word—His rule, thoughts, and will—proceeds out of our mouths, we tap into a power source that is beyond us. We access and utilize the authority of the One who spoke the creation into being and commanded the waves of the sea to be still. His authority is available to you and me if we will but believe it to be true and speak directly to whatever mountain we are facing.

We are told that when Jesus spoke God's Word to the devil, the devil had to leave (Matthew 4:11). Speaking God's truth into life's scenarios forces Satan to flee. And we all know that Satan is at the root of every issue we face.

The solution to the mountains in your life lies in what you say.

Now this truth assumes something. It assumes that you are willing to take the time to find out what God has to say about the mountain you are facing. Many Christians do not seem willing to do that. It takes too much time—perhaps they will miss too many television programs, or maybe it's easier to ask their friends or family members for their opinion. Or watch Oprah and Dr. Phil. Whatever the case, we will see the mountains in our lives move only when we couple our faith in God's will with words that reflect it.

When you are sick and you go to a medical doctor to get the medication you need, you are trusting in his authority. You may not be able to decipher his handwriting, and you might not have any idea what he is talking about when he starts listing off possible maladies. But still you will do what the doctor says simply because he has proven trustworthy. You will take the pill every day because you have come to believe the doctor. God wants us to discover what His Word says about whatever it is we are facing in our lives and then apply it. His word is like medicine to our spirit, soul, and body.

Speak to the Mountain

The week that I was preparing to preach this sermon to our local congregation, one of our members—a man I've known for some time—came to my office. He had no idea what I was preparing to teach on. He just came because he wanted to tell me about what had just happened to him at work.

Just a few days before, he had been fired from his job—not because he was doing poor work, but because of his faith as a Christian. His employer told him that the company had no tolerance for Christians at that job. People had seen him reading his Bible on his lunch hour, and they told him he couldn't do that even though he was clocked out. If he wanted to read his Bible, he would have to leave the premises.

He decided to honor his faith and the Bible, and he remained public in his confession. As a result, he was fired. While he was packing up his office and walking to his car, he prayed something like this: "Lord, You know all about this situation. I speak Your will into this situation in the name of Jesus because You know that what happened was unrighteous and unfair. You also know I need a job. So I speak a job into existence in Your name as well." Then he let it go.

Before he even made it to the car, his phone rang. A large company had found an old application of his on file and wanted to hire him. He got more money, better benefits, and a new job before he even opened his car door!

If you watch your mouth and use it rightly, you will discover a power in your palate you may not have known you had.

Of course, we don't have a similar experience in every situation, but the principle holds true. If you watch your mouth and use it rightly, you will discover a power in your palate you may not have known you had.

Are you facing a health problem? Yes, continue to go to the doctors as the Lord works through professionals to heal sickness. But at the same time, speak to your sickness and let it know that your body is healthy in Christ's name.

Are you struggling with relationship issues? Yes, make sure you have confessed any wrongdoing and forgiven those whom you need to forgive, but also speak life and harmony to that situation.

Do you have financial issues? Yes, pay your bills and look for more streams of income or ways to cut back on spending, but at the same time speak to your bank account—that it will be more than enough and then some. After all, when you are in alignment with God's rule in your life, He promises to provide for all your needs.

If you are tired of bumping into your mountain, follow Jesus's example and speak to it. Even though you may not understand how the solution could ever come about, trust that He will do it when you say it—and He will. It is done. The power in your palate is unleashed when you combine your words with faith in the Almighty, merciful God. God allows us to bring into the visible realm what He has predetermined in the spiritual realm (Isaiah 55:11).

Jesus told His disciples that the mountains they spoke to would go into the sea. Likewise, in faith, you can speak your addictions into the sea. You can speak your controlling, negative emotions into the sea. You can speak your fear and insecurity into the sea. You can speak the tension on your job right into the sea. You can speak your marital stress into the sea. You can speak that sickness into the sea. You can speak your financial woes into the sea.

Words, coupled with faith, will move mountains. They have for me. They have for many. And they will for you.

5

Victory in Your Voice

A man went to his physician one day because he thought he had a major problem. When the doctor asked him what was wrong, he told him that he hurt all over. The doctor asked the man to explain what he meant by "all over." The man proceeded to tell him that whenever he touched any part of his body, he felt pain.

The doctor was perplexed—he had never seen an ailment like this. But as he got to thinking, he considered a possibility for the problem. "Do something for me," the doctor said to the patient.

"Of course," the patient replied.

"Touch your ear," the doctor said. When the patient touched his ear, he writhed in pain. The doctor found that intriguing, so he then asked him to touch his knee. When the patient touched his knee, he had the same response. The doctor thought he might be on to something, so he asked him to touch his own knee.

"Touch your knee?" the patient asked.

"Yes, touch my knee," the doctor replied, which the patient then did. Once again, the patient writhed in pain. This validated the doctor's conclusion.

"You are not sick," the doctor stated to the patient. "What you have is a dislocated finger!"

Sometimes you may feel as if everything is wrong no matter what you do. Like this man, you might feel as if your entire life is broken. In situations like this, it seems that wherever you turn, it hurts. You are overwhelmed with your circumstances and aren't able to respond well. I'm sure we have all been in situations that appear to be unfixable—they simply run too deep, have gone on so long, and cause so much pain.

Such was the situation King Jehoshaphat found himself in in 2 Chronicles, chapter 20. In fact, it wasn't just the king who was in trouble. All of Israel was facing a problem they could not seem to fix. We are introduced to this problem in verse 1: "The Moabites and Ammonites, together with some of the Meunites, came to fight against Jehoshaphat." The king and his kingdom were surrounded by a problem they were unable to fix. They were outnumbered—several of their enemies had agreed to attack them all at once.

I would imagine that in a situation like that, the Israelites felt helpless and hopeless. A lot of emotions rise to the surface when a person feels overwhelmed, but one of the primary ones is fear. We read in verse 3, "Jehoshaphat was afraid." No matter where he looked, his kingdom was collapsing around him.

Some of us, if we were honest enough, would challenge the theological dictum that God won't put more on you than you can bear. We know what it feels like to have more put on us than we can bear. We've been burdened by life's problems, whether in our finances, our health, our family, or a relationship that just keeps going from bad to worse. Or sometimes you feel stuck in a career or job and can't see a way out of your current situation. It might be an addiction that causes you to feel trapped—surrounded on all sides, just like Jehoshaphat.

The enemy is converging on you, and you no longer feel any peace or stability in your life.

You can use your voice to gain access to the power you need to be victorious in the struggles of your life.

If you are in a situation like that or have ever been, the lessons we learn from Jehoshaphat regarding our mouth will no doubt help you immensely. The king was in a battle. He was in a war. And yet the solution to his problem—the victory he was seeking—was not found in weapons or artillery. Rather, the victory Jehoshaphat needed was found in his voice. And just as this king used his voice, you can use yours to gain access to the power you need to be victorious in the struggles of your life.

Friend, there is victory in your voice. Let's discover how you can experience it.

Look to Him

If you have ever felt powerless, you are in good company. In fact, you are keeping company with Israel's king. Listen to Jehoshaphat's words of powerlessness: "Our God, will You not judge them? For we are powerless before this vast number that comes to fight against us. We do not know what to do" (2 Chronicles 20:12).

Jehoshaphat had become weak in his knees, and his only hope at this point was a miracle. What a perfect example for us to look at when we are struggling. We can note what the king did and apply it in our own personal lives. Jehoshaphat's problem turned him toward prayer. It led him to use his mouth to talk with God. He used his lips to gain the victory he sought. Now, that's an interesting battle strategy—this king fought his war with words.

> Yahweh, the God of our ancestors, are You not the God who is in heaven, and do You not rule over all the kingdoms of the nations? Power and might are in Your hand, and no one can stand against You. Are You not our God who drove out the inhabitants of this land before Your people Israel and who gave it forever to the descendants of Abraham Your friend? They have lived in the land and have built You a sanctuary in it for Your name and have said, "If disaster comes on us—sword or judgment, pestilence or famine—we will stand before this temple and before You, for Your name is in this temple. We will cry out to You because of our distress, and You will hear and deliver" (2 Chronicles 20:6-9).

Prayer is an invitation to heaven to address something going wrong on earth. It's calling on eternity to visit time. It's giving heavenly permission for earthly intervention. Prayer is not the pregame; it is the game. It is not the preparation for battle; it is the war. Every significant movement in the history of Christianity was birthed first and foremost in prayer. That's the approach this king took when his nation was surrounded by enemies. Jehoshaphat strategically cried out to God. Let's look at the anatomy of the king's prayer.

The king begins by reminding God who He is.

Then he reminds God about what He has said.

After this, he introduces God to the problem he is facing.

The order of this prayer is important because it puts things in the proper perspective. Jehoshaphat begins by acknowledging the greatness of God—declaring His power and ability—before diving into his difficulties. When we face big problems in our lives, we need something that can give us an even bigger solution—and that something is God. You will never discover that God is all you need until God is all you have. You will learn more about God's ways and His strengths when He is the only option left on the table.

There will be times in your life when God will allow you to be overwhelmed in order to give you a bigger view of Him. I've been in those times myself. One situation in particular involved a health problem with someone I loved dearly. Through that painful time, God proved Himself stronger and bigger than the doctors and the diagnosis. My faith grew as a result, as did my intimacy with God Himself.

When a problem is so big that there is no earthly solution to fix it, you can see God work in ways that will blow your mind. This is what happened to King Jehoshaphat, and it began when the king addressed God first and foremost as great. If your view of God is small, then He will be the last resort you turn to in a difficult situation. After all, you don't really expect too much from Him. But if your view of God is great—as was the king's—you will turn to Him to deliver you, and you will begin by reminding Him of His greatness.

We can hold God hostage to His Word.

Jehoshaphat's response to his situation reveals another thing you and I can do with our mouths—we can hold God hostage to His Word. Most believers do not realize this, but you can actually hold God hostage to what He has said. You can throw His words right back at Him because He is faithful to what He has said. This is exactly what King Jehoshaphat did in his prayer. He reminded God of what He said would happen when enemies came upon them. If they would go to His house and cry out to Him, He would hear and deliver them. Essentially, Jehoshaphat said, "Remember what You said, God? Because I'm doing that right now."

I'm in my late sixties at the time of this writing, and I often get asked why I don't have to wear glasses at my age. I don't have contacts. I've never had eye surgery. I don't even wear reading glasses. But I do have a little trick that I do in order to see well. I have to do this trick because I can't see as clearly through my left eye as I can through my right eye. My left eye has some difficulties. In fact, if I were to close my right eye, everything would be blurry.

Yet my right eye is strong. It still has 20/20 vision. So even though I have a weakness in my left eye, I've learned to focus on what I see with my right eye because everything is clearer that way. My right eye more than compensates for my left eye. In other words, even though my left side is weak, my right side is strong enough to completely overcome the weakness.

Sometimes in life, one area may get weak. You may be successful in a lot of ways, such as your career, your finances, or your relationships. But there may be one area where you just can't seem to get things right regardless of what you do. In this area, you especially need to call on the strength of heaven to overrule your own weakness. You need to call on the perfection of eternity to invade the imperfection of time. King Jehoshaphat had no doubt experienced many successes in his reign, but at the time of this battle, he was facing a crisis that revealed his own weaknesses. That's why he used his mouth to call on God.

Sometimes your bus is stuck in a ditch, and you just can't get it out. But if Clark Kent is on the same bus, that changes your strategy.

If you're feeling stuck, use your lips to remind God of His greatness, His power, His strength, and His willingness to help you when you are in trouble.

This reminds me of the story of a woman who lived out in the country where there was a desperate shortage of electricity. For years she lived without electricity until finally the local utility was able to run some cables to her home so she could have electricity. However, every month her electric bill was just a few dollars. The public utility couldn't figure out why her bill was so low, so they went out to ask her if she had any problems with her electricity. When they arrived at her home, they found her on her front porch drinking lemonade. After politely introducing themselves, they asked her how often she used her electricity.

"Oh, every day!" she replied with a big smile on her face.

"Every day?" one of the gentlemen responded, perplexed by that answer.

"Yes, every day," the lady said again, curious why they wanted to know so much about her electrical use.

"Well," the other gentleman continued, "if you don't mind my asking—how long do you use it every day?"

"Just long enough to light my kerosene lantern," the elderly woman replied.

She had relied on her electricity only enough to help do things her old way. She didn't realize the electricity could be used as a new and better way for her to see at night.

Unfortunately, a lot of us turn to God and our relationship with Him in prayer only long enough to light our own human efforts to address the situations we face. We ask God to give us a little something to get us started. We come to church for an electrical charge, but when we return home, we operate according to our own human devices. Our kerosene humanity can only do so much, and we waste the greatest power in the universe, which is at our disposal through an abiding relationship with God in prayer.

Power in Praise

Jehoshaphat understood that God has the universe in His control. That's why he turned to God, the source of his solution. In 2 Chronicles 20:14, we see that immediately after Jehoshaphat addressed the problem at hand through prayer, the Spirit of the Lord came upon the prophet Jahaziel with God's response. "Listen carefully, all Judah and you inhabitants of Jerusalem, and King Jehoshaphat. This is what the LORD says: 'Do not be afraid or discouraged because of this vast number, for the battle is not yours, but God's.'"

The prophet gave Israel a specific word for a specific situation in response to a specific prayer: This battle belongs to the Lord.

When we talk about a word from God, we can be referring to three different things. Each kind of word from God has its own Greek name. This word from the Lord that Jahaziel delivered to Jehoshaphat is called a *rhema*. A *rhema* is distinct from the written Word of God (*graphe*) and the meaning of that written Word (*logos*) because *rhema* refers to a spoken word from God. It is a declaration of God's word for a particular scenario.

When Jesus was tempted by the devil in the wilderness, He spoke God's word at that moment in time—a *rhema*. When the Holy Spirit highlights a passage of Scripture to you and shows you how it applies to your specific question, that is called a *rhema*. That means if you are not sensitive to the Holy Spirit and able to discern what He is saying directly to you, you can miss God's guidance and direction in your life. If you choose not to use your lips and your voice to pray to God when you face various challenges, you could miss the victory that would be yours otherwise.

In this situation, the prophet declared God's specific instruction for Israel's battle with her enemies. Jahaziel spoke the words the Spirit led him to say. He told the Israelites that in this particular battle, they would not need to fight. Now, that's different from the approach God normally used. Most of Israel's battles included fighting, but this was a new battle, and the Israelites needed a fresh word from God.

This is a new day, so you need a fresh word from God today.

God uses different strategies for different situations. That's why you cannot rely on yesterday's strategy for today's problem. God had a reason for wanting you to do things a certain way yesterday, but this is a new day, so you need a fresh word from God today.

This was God's instruction to the Israelites:

> Tomorrow, go down against them. You will see them coming up the Ascent of Ziz, and you will find them at the end of the valley facing the Wilderness of Jeruel. You do not have to fight this battle. Position yourselves, stand still, and see the salvation of the LORD. He is with you, Judah and Jerusalem. Do not be afraid or discouraged. Tomorrow, go out to face them, for Yahweh is with you (2 Chronicles 20:16-17).

This time, the Israelites were not called upon to fight. In this battle, they merely had to station themselves.

In a football game, when a quarterback hands off the ball to a running back, he removes himself from the chase. In this battle, God told the Israelites to hand the battle off to God, and He would handle it. As a result, Jehoshaphat "bowed with his face to the ground, and all Judah and the inhabitants of Jerusalem fell down before the LORD to worship Him" (verse 18).

The king and his countrymen worshipped God. In fact, they began to praise God with a very loud voice. Scripture continues, "Then the Levites from the sons of the Kohathites and the Korahites stood up to praise the LORD God of Israel shouting with a loud voice" (verse 19). Not only that, but the next morning they woke up and got their praise on as well.

> In the morning they got up early and went out to the wilderness of Tekoa. As they were about to go out, Jehoshaphat stood and said, "Hear me, Judah and you inhabitants of Jerusalem. Believe in Yahweh your God, and you will be established; believe in His prophets, and you will succeed." Then he consulted with the people and appointed some to sing for the LORD and some to praise the splendor of His holiness. When they went out in front of the armed forces, they kept singing:
> "Give thanks to the LORD,
>   for His faithful love endures forever"
>   (2 Chronicles 20:20-21).

When the Israelites began singing and praising God, God set ambushes against their enemies (verses 22-23). The Lord gained their victory in response to the praise of their lips, just as He said He would. Their problem had led them to pray, which resulted in a prophet's message. His words brought about praise, which led to the victory.

If you ever want to know God's address—where He lives—it's found in Psalm 22:3. He is "enthroned on the praises" of His people. Or take a look at Isaiah 60:18, where we read that His gates are praise.

Praise is a visible and verbal expression of how you feel about God.

What is praise? Praise is the visible, verbal expression of worship. It is the expression of adoration of who God is and what He has done or what we are trusting Him to do. Worship can be silent, but praise is always audible. Compare it to getting saved and being a disciple. You can get saved all by yourself with no one else knowing, but you can't be a disciple in private. A disciple is someone who goes public and declares Christ as Lord. Similarly, praise is a visible and verbal expression of how you feel about God.

For example, a man may love his wife but never say so. It's like the man whose wife complained that he never said, "I love you." He replied that he had said it 15 years ago, and if it ever changed, he'd let her know. That approach won't work in marriage, and it also won't work in our relationship with the Lord. Authentic praise to God comes out of an abiding heart that is willing to hang out in His presence. God wants to hear and feel your praise. Your praise is where your deliverance is found (Psalm 50:23).

Friend, never allow yourself to be too cute or too sophisticated to praise God. There is nothing special about keeping your praise inside you. Give God the pleasure of not only knowing your worship but also hearing how much He means to you. Give Him the delight of experiencing your trust in Him.

Most people have no problem offering verbal praise when they attend a sporting event. In fact, when the home team makes a great play and someone stays in their seat, most people wonder what's wrong with that person. You are supposed to cheer. You are supposed to praise. You are supposed to verbalize the greatness of what just went on.

The same is true with God. Sometimes we don't notice the incredible things God has done, and that could be one reason why we are occasionally reluctant to praise Him openly. But He is worthy of our praise on every level.

One of the most strategic uses of your mouth is to praise God—and to praise Him often. That could be at church in corporate praise, or it could be in your car as you sing along to praise songs. It could be in the words you use in conversation, or it could be in the words you speak to yourself when you're doing chores around the house. Let praise continually be in your heart and on your lips as you give God the glory that is due Him.

And when you feel down and your struggles are tough, you can still praise. Let your praise be a sacrifice, as it is called in Hebrews 13:15. Sometimes it's difficult to see the good in a situation, just as it was for the Israelites when their enemies surrounded them. In those times, offering praise is truly a sacrifice. You are praising God in faith despite the pain and confusion you feel. You are honoring God in trust despite the calamity that surrounds you. And when you express your worship in praise—especially in those hard times—the Lord hears your heart and rewards the authenticity of your praise with His presence.

Victory in Your Voice

As Job said following the loss of his fortune and family, "The LORD gives, and the LORD takes away. Praise the name of Yahweh" (Job 1:21). Through it all, Job did not lose his faith in God, and he never stopped giving God praise. And because of that, Job not only regained what he had lost but also gained a new experience of God's reality and a new level of His favor and provision.

The same is true for the Israelites and their king. When they chose to give God praise in obedience and in faith during their battle, they received the victory they were promised. The Scripture clearly ties their victory to their voice by giving us the exact timing that each took place. It was precisely when God heard their praise that they received His hand of intervention in their war. Not a moment before and not a moment after. God synchronized His deliverance with their praise.

> The moment they began their shouts and praises, the LORD set an ambush against the Ammonites, Moabites, and the inhabitants of Mount Seir who came to fight against Judah, and they were defeated. The Ammonites and Moabites turned against the inhabitants of Mount Seir and completely annihilated them. When they had finished with the inhabitants of Seir, they helped destroy each other (2 Chronicles 20:22-23).

You can utter your praise in a whisper or in a shout—it makes little difference. The difference comes in the act of offering it in faith. When you are facing a crisis you cannot overcome—whether it's an addiction or a crisis in your emotions, relationships, finances, or health—use your mouth to give God praise. Let God hear your praise because God knows that your enemies cannot withstand your praise.

Before Satan fell, he led all the angels in the act of giving praise. His job was to lead the worship of God. We could call him the praise and worship leader of heaven. But one day Satan looked in a mirror and said, "Mirror, mirror on the wall, who is the fairest of them all?" He then answered himself that he was the fairest, and he went on a mission of making himself like the Most High.

One-third of the angels joined Satan in his rebellion, and there has been a competition for our praise ever since. Each and every moment of his existence, Satan illegitimately seeks to transfer our praise—which is legitimately due to God—to himself. So when God hears your praise, and especially when circumstances would tempt you to remain silent, He honors your faith (Hebrews 11:1). He takes care of your issues. He defeats your enemies. He delivers you from your bondage. And He wins your battle.

This is similar to when the Lord told the army commander Joshua to circle the impregnable Jericho wall six times—once a day for six days. On the seventh day, God's people were to shout (Joshua 6:3-5). When they obeyed, their voices drew down their victory. Their praise tore down that wall. Their shout defeated the undefeatable enemy (verse 20).

God responds to the praise of His people.

In Acts 16, the Bible recounts another experience of people's voices leading the way to victory. At midnight, Paul and Silas were chained in a dark prison. However, when they began to praise God and give voice to His glory, the ground began to shake. As these two men praised God with their voices, the cell doors opened, and they were set free (verses 25-26).

God responds to the praise of His people.

Praise is the most powerful weapon you possess. Let Psalm 34:1-3 be your battle cry: "I will praise the LORD at all times; His praise will always be on my lips. I will boast in the LORD; the humble will hear and be glad. Proclaim Yahweh's greatness with me; let us exalt His name together."

The NASB renders verse 3, "O magnify the LORD with me." Keep in mind that when you magnify something, you don't make the object itself bigger. Rather, you make it look bigger to you. God is already as big as He will ever be. But far too often, we put Him in a box, minimize His presence in our lives, and forget that He not only created the universe but also rules it. When you and I choose to give God praise regardless of what is happening all around us, we increase our view of God in our own eyes, heart, and mind. We give Him the glory that is due His name.

Will you take a moment to do that right now? Wherever you are, give God praise. It doesn't have to be loud—just sincere.

When I preached on this subject in our church recently, I invited the congregation to stay after the service as long as they wanted. We would leave the lights on and the doors open. Thousands of people remained, giving God praise. An hour passed, and people were still giving God praise. It was a powerful moment in the life of our church and its members, and I know your praise will open the door to a powerful moment in your own life. You hold the power to reverse any negative situation in your life right now simply by surrendering your heart in faith to the Lord and giving Him praise.

Are you ready to use your voice to claim the victory that is yours?

6

Wisdom in Your Words

A treacherous road is wrapped around the shoreline of the Pacific Coast like a scarf around a neck. Mountains and cliffs zigzag here and there, and the road zigzags with them. Sharp curves appear suddenly, as if in a video game. Warning signs alert drivers to slow down for the most dangerous sections.

Such signs stand bravely, warning drivers of curves, animal crossings, and falling rocks. They dot the landscape of Route 1 on the California coast and are almost as plentiful as nature itself. The signs have been put there in abundance to give drivers guidance as they maneuver the precarious highway.

The more difficult and dangerous our pathway is, the more we need guidance.

Life is sometimes treacherous. Twists and turns come our way without warning. Unexpected circumstances and events frequently pop up on our path. Unless we know how to navigate such difficult terrain in life, we can easily go over a cliff.

The Bible tells us what we need in order to negotiate the twists and turns of life—wisdom.

Wisdom can be defined as the skill of accurately applying spiritual truths to life's various situations. Scripture's antonym for wisdom is foolishness. A fool is a person who refuses to apply God's perspective to life's decisions. When a godless mind is combined with a wide mouth, foolish speech will be the result. Wisdom and foolishness are often contrasted with each other in the Bible, and one of the ways this shows up the most is with regard to our speech, especially in the book of Proverbs. I could list a great number of verses, but let me start with a few:

- "The tongue of the wise makes knowledge attractive,
  but the mouth of fools blurts out foolishness" (15:2).

- "The tongue that heals is a tree of life,
  but a devious tongue breaks the spirit" (15:4).

- "The lips of the wise broadcast knowledge,
  but not so the heart of fools" (15:7).

- "Wisdom is found on the lips of the discerning,
  but a rod is for the back of the one who lacks sense.
  The wise store up knowledge,
  but the mouth of the fool hastens destruction" (10:13-14).

- "When there are many words, sin is unavoidable,
  but the one who controls his lips is wise.
  The tongue of the righteous is pure silver;
  the heart of the wicked is of little value.
  The lips of the righteous feed many,
  but fools die for lack of sense" (10:19-21).

These verses and many others make clear that if you could be wiser with your speech, life would be better. God tells us that when we are foolish with our speech, life doesn't go so well.

Talk better, and you will live better.

Talk poorly, and your life will follow that similar path.

As I mentioned earlier, wisdom is the skill of applying spiritual truth to life's choices. But to speak with wisdom, you must have two other things in play. First, you must have knowledge. You need an accurate base of information from which to draw. If you are working with a flawed information base and your knowledge is skewed, then your reasoning and your decisions will be messed up as well. Just as your computer requires good data to provide the correct output, you need good data to make good decisions about what to say. If your input is wrong, what you say will be wrong as well. You won't be speaking with wisdom.

Have you ever been talking with someone when suddenly, halfway through the conversation, you get some new information that entirely changes the way you view the situation? What you had determined prior to receiving this information no longer applies because your new knowledge has changed your response. In times like these you may say, "Oh, that changes things," or "That makes sense now in light of the additional information."

This is why it's critical to seek truth as a knowledge base for wisdom and why Scripture tells us, "The fear of the LORD is the beginning of wisdom, and the knowledge of the Holy One is understanding" (Proverbs 9:10). You can't be sure your information is accurate unless you first start with God. Starting with God and His viewpoint can save you a lot of time as well.

The second thing you need in order to speak with wisdom is understanding. We read in Proverbs 4:7, "Wisdom is supreme—so get wisdom. And whatever else you get, get understanding." Knowledge has to do with information, but understanding has to do with the meaning of the information. When you are able to combine knowledge and understanding together accurately, you end up with wisdom.

For example, many people know the basic skills for using a

computer and some common applications, such as photo-editing software. But if you were like me, you wouldn't know how to use a computer at all. Granted, you would have general knowledge of the computer and software, yet the understanding of how to apply that knowledge personally would be lacking. Because of that, you would be unable to fully maximize the computer and the software.

Wisdom involves more than being smart. You can have multiple degrees and still be a fool. Wisdom is the ability to see beyond the obvious and make choices that reflect the highest good for everyone involved, including yourself.

This reminds me of the story of four people on an airplane that lost an engine and was about to go down. Unfortunately there were only three parachutes on the plane. The pilot was the first to grab a parachute—he said he had a wife and two kids, so he needed to live. Next, a man who was known as a genius looked at the other two and said he needed a parachute so the world could benefit from his brilliant mind.

This left a minister and a kid. The minister turned to the kid and told him he had lived a full life, that he was not afraid of death and would be willing to meet his Maker. So he offered the parachute to the kid. The kid just smiled and said, "That's okay, sir. There are still two parachutes left—the genius just grabbed my backpack and jumped."

You can be smart but not know the difference between a parachute and a backpack. Only when knowledge and understanding come together is wisdom born.

———————————————

A foolish mouth is one of the most destructive things on the planet.

———————————————

A lot of trouble is caused by a lack of wisdom. In fact, a foolish mouth is one of the most destructive things on the planet. When people don't speak with wisdom, chaos ensues. A few more verses remind us of this.

- "A fool's lips lead to strife,
  and his mouth provokes a beating" (Proverbs 18:6).
- "Better a poor man who lives with integrity
  than someone who has deceitful lips and is a fool"
  (Proverbs 19:1).

Scripture warns us not to entertain a fool but to answer him simply: "Answer a fool according to his foolishness or he'll become wise in his own eyes" (Proverbs 26:5). In other words, never encourage a fool. Rather, respond wisely.

The famous preacher John Wesley is said to have been walking down the street one day when a man who opposed him stood in front of him and would not move. Wesley asked why, and the man replied, "Because I never get out of the way for a fool."

Wesley thought for a minute and then replied, "Well, I do," and then proceeded to step to the side and go around him.

The fool is not choosing the best way. The fool is merely choosing his own way. "There is a way that seems right to a man, but its end is the way to death" (Proverbs 14:12).

Seek Wisdom

As we grow in our relationships with each other through the wise use of our mouths, the idea is to discover how to get more wisdom today than we had yesterday. Wisdom is so critical that it can steer you through the pathways of life, telling you to make a turn here and not make a turn there, what to choose here and what not to choose

there, what person is good here and what person is not so good there.
Therefore we should make seeking wisdom a regular part of our lives.

The most extensive passage in the Bible on wisdom is Job 28:12-28:

> But where can wisdom be found,
> and where is understanding located?
> No man can know its value,
> since it cannot be found in the land of the living.
> The ocean depths say, "It's not in me,"
> while the sea declares, "I don't have it."
> Gold cannot be exchanged for it,
> and silver cannot be weighed out for its price.
> Wisdom cannot be valued in the gold of Ophir,
> in precious onyx or sapphire.
> Gold and glass do not compare with it,
> and articles of fine gold cannot be exchanged for it.
> Coral and quartz are not worth mentioning.
> The price of wisdom is beyond pearls.
> Topaz from Cush cannot compare with it,
> and it cannot be valued in pure gold.
> Where then does wisdom come from,
> and where is understanding located?
> It is hidden from the eyes of every living thing
> and concealed from the birds of the sky.
> Abaddon and Death say,
> "We have heard news of it with our ears."
> But God understands the way to wisdom,
> and He knows its location.
> For He looks to the ends of the earth
> and sees everything under the heavens.
> When God fixed the weight of the wind
> and limited the water by measure,
> when He established a limit for the rain

and a path for the lightning,
He considered wisdom and evaluated it;
He established it and examined it.
He said to mankind,
"The fear of the Lord is this: wisdom.
And to turn from evil is understanding."

Job begins his soliloquy by asking a very common and important question. If wisdom is so critical to a life well lived, where can it be found? Where can we locate it? The first answer to that question is that man neither fully understands its value nor contains it in himself. Looking for wisdom in people, the sea, and the creation will not produce it. You may find information in those things, but you will not find the guidance you need to make right choices.

Wisdom is so valuable that gold cannot be exchanged for it, nor can it be bought. The answer to Job's question, which is also our question, is found in the final verse. The fear of the Lord is wisdom. He established wisdom. He creates it. He defines it. God alone is wisdom, just as God alone is love. When these qualities show up in our lives, they are reflections and manifestations of God's image in us.

Apart from God, wisdom does not exist. If you and I want to know how to say the word that will sustain the weary, move mountains, and heal people's wounds, we need wisdom that comes only from God. The reason why God knows everything and is the only One who does, is that He eternally exists in the present tense. As we read in His revelation to Moses, "I AM WHO I AM" (Exodus 3:14). God doesn't have a yesterday, nor does He have a tomorrow. Everything is "now" to Him. There is no night to God, nor is there day. Everything is expressed and experienced in its fullness.

When God says something is going to happen tomorrow, He is not waiting for it to happen tomorrow. He has already been to tomorrow. He cannot doubt or make a wrong decision. God knows all the contingencies. He doesn't have to guess. When you take God seriously, you will get wisdom. But when you skip God and His viewpoint on a matter, you wind up talking like a fool.

The Gift of Wisdom

God makes us a promise about wisdom in the book of James. This is one of the most straightforward promises of the Bible: "Now if any of you lacks wisdom, he should ask God, who gives to all generously and without criticizing, and it will be given to him" (James 1:5). Wisdom is your birthright, your inheritance, your gift...and it's free. All you have to do is ask God, and He promises to give you wisdom. God will give you wisdom on how to talk, act, think, and even believe. He can even give you wisdom in the moment you need it. As we saw in chapter 3, God can show up at a time when you need Him the most and give you just the right words to diffuse a situation or create a breakthrough. But this requires that you surrender to Him, receive His thoughts, and abide in His presence so you are in a position of asking.

God can give you wisdom in the moment you need it.

King Solomon once faced a challenging situation involving two mothers with one live baby and one dead baby. Both mothers came to him and claimed to be the mother of the live baby. Solomon needed to discern which mother was telling the truth (1 Kings 3:16-28).

God gave Solomon the wisdom to respond by suggesting that the live baby simply be cut in half and given to both mothers. At that point, one of the women came forward to relinquish her child and allow the other mother to claim the baby. That is when Solomon knew the answer to his question. He gave the live baby to the mother who was willing to give it up so it could live.

God can give you wise words in everyday life situations, just as He gave Solomon wise words. He can help you to know exactly what to say to that coworker who offends you or tries to block your forward progress. He can give you the right words to say to your boss to open up more freedom and responsibility in your work. God can guide you on what to say to your spouse to draw the two of you closer together. Or to your child, to a friend...even, and perhaps most importantly, to yourself.

Wisdom is a priceless gift from God that far too often goes unopened. To witness God's supernatural power flowing out from your own lips is one of the greatest blessings of life. When you hear yourself say something or respond to something in a way that you could not have on your own, you experience God at a greater level than ever before. The more you experience this, the more natural and comfortable it will be for you to rely on Him in that way. Before you know it, your first move will be to check with God before opening your mouth. Why not, when He is so willing to give you wisdom when you ask?

One day a son went to his father with a problem. He had loaned a friend $500, but his friend had not yet paid him back. So much time had passed, he thought his friend had actually forgotten. No paper was signed, and he had given his friend cash, so he was concerned that he wouldn't be able to prove his friend owed him the money.

"That's not a problem," his dad replied. "Just text your friend that you'd like the $1000 you loaned him back. When he texts you back that it was only $500, you've got it in writing!"

Wisdom finds solutions where you thought there were none. You and I have a heavenly Father who willingly gives us these solutions and more if we only ask. Make it a habit to begin each day with a request for wisdom in your words. It doesn't have to be a long prayer, just a sincere one. God desires to dispense wisdom into your communication, thus affecting your choices in life. He wants you to be wise—to have both knowledge and understanding—so that your speech brings glory to Him, good to others, and blessing to yourself.

Ministry in Your Mouth

If you have ever been to Las Vegas, you've surely been astonished at the sheer size and grandeur of the buildings in this desert city. I have driven through the city with my family on road trips headed out west, and it never ceases to astonish me how many buildings can go up so quickly in this one area.

Yet you may not be aware that demolishing buildings in Vegas has become an attraction of its own. It began around 1993 when the first old building, the Dunes, was imploded in order to make room for a new one, the Bellagio.[3] The event was such a spectacle that people drove from miles around to witness it. Since then these massive implosions have continued to draw crowds and have taken on a life of their own, complete with fireworks, news cameras, music, and a show!

Vegas has found a way to twist the destructive nature of implosions into a party as only Vegas could. But implosions in our lives—whether in our relationships, families, hopes, dreams, careers, health, or more—typically come wrapped with sorrow and laced with loss. And they also typically come by way of the mouth.

Just as an implosion takes only minutes to bring down what required years to erect, our words have the power to destroy each other and even ourselves as soon as they're spoken. But in this chapter, I want to focus on the opposite of tearing each other down. I want to look at what the Scripture says we can do build one another up. Your mouth has the power to destroy, but it also has the power to create, and one primary method that is used for this is the process we call edification.

Build Each Other Up

Commands to edify one another and build each other up are given over and over throughout God's Word. Here are a few examples.

- "So then, we must pursue what promotes peace and what builds up one another" (Romans 14:19).

- "All things must be done for edification" (1 Corinthians 14:26).

- "From Him the whole body, fitted and knit together by every supporting ligament, promotes the growth of the body for building up itself in love by the proper working of each individual part" (Ephesians 4:16).

- "Therefore encourage one another and build each other up as you are already doing" (1 Thessalonians 5:11).

Our role in the body of Christ, our goal in our relationships, involves this process of building each other up. One of the primary ways we do this is with our mouths—the words we say, post, text, and pray. When people in your home, at your job, in your church, or in your neighborhood come into your presence, do they sense that you are building them up or tearing them down? Far too many churches are known for a spirit of judgment and destruction rather than a spirit of love, grace, and edification. Yet the Bible is clear that in the environment of God's presence, we—the members of His family—are to be construction workers who build people up rather than the demolition crew that destroys.

One key verse in the Bible tells us how we are to go about this process of edification. In Ephesians 4:29 (NASB) we read, "Let no unwholesome word proceed from your mouth, but only such a word as is good for edification according to the need of the moment, so that it will give grace to those who hear." In this passage, God specifically ties edification to communication. We edify each other by what we say and how we say it, as well as by what we do not say.

Words that people speak to each other matter greatly. How many times have you repeated something in your head that someone said to you earlier that day or that week? That person may have said those words to you or about you without giving them much thought, but in your mind, they have grown into a monster you can't get rid of. Words affect what we think, how we feel, and how we act.

If a judge says "guilty" or "innocent," those words matter. If a doctor says to you "benign" or "malignant," trust me, those words matter. Words affect our well-being because they are a linguistic reflection of realities, belief systems, and thoughts.

A woman came to her pastor one day and said, "Pastor, I want to put my tongue on the altar."

The pastor replied, "My friend, our altar is not that big."

When it comes to giving our communication to God, that is something larger than we may have even imagined.

Another lady shared that when she decided to give up gossip, she literally had nothing to say to herself or her friends for three full weeks. Gossip had become such a habitual way of thinking and relating that it took that long to simply figure out what else to talk about.

A husband and wife were driving down the road one day and saw some mules grazing in a pasture. The husband turned to the wife and cuttingly remarked, "There go your relatives."

The wife took no time with her reply. "I know—by marriage."

When we look at some of the ways words can unravel relationships, we will see how absolutely intentional we must be with such powerful tools. The purpose of your mouth is to build up.

Graciousness can turn your speech into something remarkable.

Season with Salt

As Paul wrote in Colossians 4:6, "Your speech should always be gracious, seasoned with salt, so that you may know how you should answer each person." Keep in mind that Paul used the word "always" to indicate how often our speech should be seasoned with grace. Just as salt can change the taste of a french fry, turning it from plain potato into something incredible, graciousness can turn your speech into something remarkable.

God doesn't want your speech to be bland. He wants it to be flavored with the goodness of His grace. But just as in cooking, seasoning in your speech must be intentional. Food isn't seasoned by mistake. Seasoning is used knowingly, and usually to taste. A master chef will season the food and then taste it, going back and forth until it is just right. God wants you and me to do the same with our speech—to make it tasty and life-giving to those who hear it.

Grace is the favor of God. So whenever you speak, seek the high ground to know what to say and how to say it. Always season your words with grace. One of the reasons people used to season their food with salt was to prevent it from decaying. Similarly, speech that is flavored with grace prevents decay in our relationships, dreams, and much more. Gracious speech preserves everyone involved.

When you are not preserving something through what you say, you are contributing to its decay. You can choose to use your mouth for life or for death, but those are your only options. God has set it up that way. Your words will create life or bring in death whether you are aware of it or not.

How you say what you say is often just as important as what you say.

Consider the husband who was looking after his wife's elderly mother, who was living with them at the time, along with his wife's dog, whom his wife loved very much. His wife needed to run out and do some errands. She came back a few hours later and asked, "Where's the dog?"

Her husband replied, "The dog is dead."

"What?" she shrieked. "I can't believe you just blurted that out! Can't you try to be a little more sympathetic? You could have softened your words a little, maybe by saying, 'The dog was on the roof...it slipped and fell...I did all I could, but he didn't make it.'"

After the man's wife recovered a little, she noticed she hadn't seen her mother. So she asked her husband, "Where's my mother?"

The husband thought for a moment and then replied, "Well, your mom was on the roof..."

Are you too direct in your speech? Is there room for you to soften what you say? Are you perfecting the art of being polite when talking with those around you? Too many relationships today are punctuated with harsh talk.

Another aspect of salt is that it makes you thirsty. When I'm at an airport and have some time to spend before boarding my plane, I usually wait in the Admiral's Club and read or make some phone calls. Without fail, I'm asked if I would like something to drink. I always reply, "Yes, please, a ginger ale." My drink arrives with a bowl full of salty snacks. The Admiral's Club marketers realize that the more salty food I eat, the more drinks I will order.

Season your speech with God's grace, and
people will come back to you for more.

The same thing is true with your speech. Season your speech with God's grace, and people will come back to you for more. They will listen intently to your words, and your voice will give life and peace to those around you. Likewise, when God sees you using your lips to produce life, He will communicate to you and through your mouth to others. He will give you the wisdom to know how to respond to life's delicate moments.

God is a God of grace, so if you are speaking without grace, He will not participate in your communication. Rather, you will be speaking from the limited resources of your humanity—or worse, from satanic influence. God does not operate outside of His own character, so to invite God into your words, mouth, language, and conversation, you must align your heart, thoughts, and speech with who He is.

Words That Help, Words That Heal

If we are to intervene in the muck and mire of other people's lives in an effort to make a difference, we are going to have to transform our minds and recognize the importance of the role of edification.

Yes, when other people's hopelessness seems overwhelming to us, as it can, you may wonder how they could ever overcome it. But if you will edify, build up, and encourage them, they can. Remember, no situation is so far gone that God cannot redeem it. And that's what we need to remind each other regularly—to keep the faith, hold on, not throw in the towel...to hope as Abraham did even when he had no hope at all. "In hope against all hope he believed" (Romans 4:18 NASB). God will honor their trust, and He will honor you for using your mouth, your texts, your social media posts, your prayers, and more to remind others to hope in Him. He can turn their emotional pain into victorious gain—and use your mouth in the process.

I'll never forget a particularly taxing time in my life when the routine of ministry caught up with me and I began to wonder, "Is this even worth it? Does all this preparation for a message on Sunday even make a difference?" After all, I would talk to people on Tuesday or Wednesday, and they couldn't remember the subject of my sermon on Sunday. If you hear that enough times, you begin to wonder whether what you are doing really matters.

But God knew the struggle of my heart, and about that time an anonymous person began texting me from an unfamiliar number each Sunday morning. The text wouldn't be long, but it always included an encouraging Bible verse. You have no idea how much that meant to me. I felt as if God Himself were texting me, reminding me that what I did made a difference and encouraging me to hang in there, to keep going, and to continue doing what He had called me to do.

You never know how powerful your words
can be in someone else's life.

Friend, you never know how powerful your words can be in someone else's life. Often, God will prompt you to say or send something to someone without really knowing what is going on in their lives. But God knows, and He is asking you to be the vehicle of encouragement. "A word spoken at the right time is like gold apples on a silver tray" (Proverbs 25:11).

You can sharpen your own edification skills by recognizing what edifies you and builds you up. Think about what others say to you that lifts you up the most when you are feeling down. Then look for opportunities to say similar things to someone else in your life. It could be speaking words of affirmation, texting a Bible verse, praying with someone, or providing a listening ear with a closed mouth.

Also, keep in mind that everyone likes to be spoken of highly at some time or another. One way to incorporate the virtue of edification into your life is to always include a positive statement about someone when you introduce him or her to someone else. Try establishing this as a habit in your life and relationships.

Also, rather than asking, "How can I help?" try asking, "Would it help if I…?" This can edify someone at a greater level. You are accepting responsibility to supply the encouragement rather than requiring the other person to come up with something for you to do. You are also saving them from feeling like they are bothering you when they do think of something you can do.

Being Present

Use your words to build a blessing in someone's life by being intentional, specific, authentic, and present.

Being present is a lost art in our culture these days—including in the workplace. Not too long ago, during a meeting of our ministry leaders, I noticed that some individuals were picking up their phones or tablets. Rather than being truly present with each other, they were essentially going somewhere else. I'm sure others would have noticed if I sat at the head of the table and did the same thing, but apparently they thought nothing of doing it themselves.

What would happen, I wondered, if I stood up to preach but then got out my phone and started texting someone or reading posts on social media? I imagine most people would say I should put my phone back in my pocket where it belongs. Why? Because they had come to hear me preach, and I cannot preach if I am not present. And yet how many times do we sit down to lunch or dinner with family or friends, or at a meeting at work, and casually pick up our phones and go somewhere else?

Edification involves more than what you say. It involves being present enough to listen and then know how to respond. When you spend time with people, make sure to put away any distractions and give them your full presence. It is not a sign of importance or significance to constantly be on the phone while in the presence of others. Actually, it is a sign of low self-esteem—you are revealing you do not value yourself enough to believe you have something to offer to those around you.

Speaking the Truth in Love

Being spiritual has nothing to do with the degrees on your wall or how much education you have. It has nothing to do with how old you are either. A person could be 90 years old but have lived carnally for those 90 years. You can be a high school dropout and still be more spiritual than a person with a master's degree in theology. Being spiritual means living every area of your life underneath the comprehensive rule of God. It means aligning your thoughts and words with His own. When you do that, edifying others will not be difficult because we serve a God of hope, second chances, and grace.

When your speech contains both truth and love, you
are living as a mature believer in Christ.

Some Christians seem to focus more on telling the truth than
on sharing the love. Paul tells us in Ephesians 4:15 that we are to
have both in our speech: "Speaking the truth in love, let us grow in
every way into Him who is the head—Christ." When your speech
contains both truth and love, you are living as a mature believer in
Christ.

You can tell someone the truth without caring about them. At the
end of the conversation, they will have heard the truth, but they may
react negatively—not so much to the information you gave them,
but to you. As a result, they will be worse off than they were before
rather than better.

Or your words can convey empty sentimentalism but little or no
truth. They may make people feel good for the moment, but your
words will not build up because they were not based on the founda-
tion of truth.

If you don't tell someone the truth, you don't help them. If you
tell someone the truth without a spirit of love, you don't help them
then either. The art of edification is the skillful combining of both
truth and love so that the other person receives the right information
from the right heart.

As we saw in the verse that opened this chapter, Ephesians 4:29,
our speech is a ministry. It is a ministry because it "gives grace to those
who hear." Grace is unmerited, divine favor. So the person hearing
your words may not necessarily deserve the grace you are giving them,
but that's exactly what grace is. That's exactly what God gives to us in

so many ways—His grace. And yet we often turn around and dole out destruction to others in what we say.

Paul tells us that in doing so we cause the Holy Spirit great pain. We grieve Him. "And don't grieve God's Holy Spirit," Paul writes. "You were sealed by Him for the day of redemption. All bitterness, anger and wrath, shouting and slander must be removed from you, along with all malice" (Ephesians 4:30-31). So if your tongue hurts someone, you have made the Holy Spirit sad inside you. If the Holy Spirit is sad inside you, He is not in a position to help you strongly because of the relational distance between you and Him.

The opposite of that is true as well. As you build up blessings in other people's lives through this process called edification, you will be inviting blessings from the Spirit into your own life.

Speech is a powerful tool. Test it out today and this week. When you are tempted to say something negative to someone, do the reverse and speak words that build up. Then watch how the Lord responds in your own life as well. He is faithful. As you serve Him by helping others, you will recognize His presence manifested more fully and tangibly in and for you.

8

Thanksgiving in Your Throat

You and I live today in what I call a world of saccharine celebrities. These are celebrity substitutes—people who are paraded before us as winners. Our culture and our society are captivated by award shows, including the Oscars, Emmys, Grammys, Tonys, and ESPYs. We applaud the performances of famous people who show up in business, athletics, and on screen. These individuals are often seen as heroes.

If you define a celebrity as someone who has reached a high status of fame, power, ability, position, or money, then I'd like to remind us of the greatest celebrity of all. God is the celebrity of the universe in His own unique way. He's not like our modern heroes—hot today and cold tomorrow. Neither is He replaceable, as all other celebrities are. Nobody is greater, and no one can take His place. God doesn't grow old, His hair doesn't thin, He never loses His speed, and His gifts and skills don't diminish with time. He is forever the Almighty One.

Throughout Scripture, we are given many injunctions with regard to this greatest of all celebrities, but I want to focus on one instruction as we wrap up our time together studying the power of the mouth. In 1 Thessalonians 5:18 we read, "Give thanks in everything, for this is God's will for you in Christ Jesus."

What does it mean to give thanks? Thanksgiving may simply be defined as the recognition of God's goodness with a heart of gratitude. It is expressing in word and deed your gratitude to God for being the source of all your blessings. Thanksgiving starts with the premise that God Himself is your source. When you remember that every opportunity, blessing, or goodness that comes to you has come from God and not from man, your heart will be grateful to Him. Far too often we give mankind thanks for what God has done.

As soon as children learn to speak, their parents teach them the importance of saying "thank you." God's heart desires the same from us. Thanksgiving includes more than the words you say. It is a worldview, a mindset. You don't say "thanks" one time in the morning and then consider yourself covered for the whole day. How would you feel if your child thanked you one time in the morning but never expressed appreciation throughout the day? God wants our hearts to beat to the cadence of thanks. He wants thanksgiving to be our ongoing way of life.

Failure to give thanks is an insult to the Almighty God.

When we fail to give thanks, we imply that we are the source of the good things that come our way. This is an insult to the Almighty God.

Whatever we receive, we are to receive it with a heart of thanks. As we read in 1 Timothy 4:4, "Everything created by God is good, and nothing should be rejected if it is received with thanksgiving." Everything created by God is good. Unfortunately, we often try to police God rather than receiving what He has given us with a spirit and statement of thanks. We try to box in God instead of allowing Him to expand our horizons with His plans.

Nothing should be rejected if it is received with a heart of thanks and comes from the hand of God Himself. James puts it this way: "Every generous act and every perfect gift is from above, coming down from the Father of lights; with Him there is no variation or shadow cast by turning" (James 1:17).

It is very interesting that the Old Testament has no Hebrew word that specifically means "thanks." The Hebrew way of showing gratitude to God included pouring out a voluminous amount of words. One word can't catch it all. It's too big, too powerful, and too deep. Thus we are given a variety of words and concepts in Hebrew that all have to do with the expression of gratitude.

Yadah is one of the Hebrew words the translators rendered as "thanks," but it literally means to talk about how wonderful someone is or about a great thing they did. The Israelites thanked someone by spreading a good report about the person.

Another Hebrew word that communicates thanks in the Old Testament is the word we often translate as "hallelujah." Hallelujah is a combination of two words: *hallalu*, which means "praise," and *Jah*, which is short for Yahweh. Put together, these words mean, "Praise God!"

We looked at praise in chapter 5, so I'll just add a brief reminder here. We shout out our praise for a sports team that just won the big game, and we applaud a celebrity who walks in our midst. God is looking for us to give Him legitimate praise and thanksgiving from our lips. That's what His heart desires and what He deserves.

After all, the ordinary things God does are far greater than the super-extraordinary things man can do.

This emotional response to how great God is ought to be one of the primary uses of our mouths. "I will praise the LORD at all times; His praise will always be on my lips" (Psalm 34:1). The NASB puts it this way: "His praise shall continually be in my mouth." How often is continually? All the time. After all, how often does God give you breath? So it makes sense that our praise of Him should comprise the greatest volume of what comes out of our mouths.

God wants to be blessed by your lips. He wants to hear your gratitude and thanksgiving. You bless Him when you remember what He has done for you and express your appreciation to Him and to others.

I used to have a dog. I fed that dog faithfully. I changed its water bowl every single day. That dog never once told me thanks. In fact, one time when I went to feed the dog, he growled at me as I set the food bowl down next to him. Which is exactly why I opened this paragraph with "I used to have a dog." Things don't work that way in my house. If you want to stay in my house, no growling is allowed, and you better come with some thanks.

Now that's just me, a human being. Can you imagine how God must feel when He constantly doles out our provision—day in and day out—and rarely gets thanked? Then, when we feel as if something has gone wrong, we growl and complain at the One who has done and is doing so much for us!

Friend, watch your mouth. Replace complaining with thanksgiving. It is the right thing to do. Ingratitude and complaining distance us from God. As a result, we lose out on experiencing many of the blessings God has prepared for us, and we experience His discipline instead (Numbers 11:1; 1 Corinthians 10:10; James 5:9).

Don't be a Kibbles 'n Bits believer who forgets the Source of all you have. Nothing you have comes from you. The money you spend comes from God. The skills you have come from God. The house you live in—it came from God. Even the air you breathe comes from God. He is your Source. So do yourself a favor and thank Him continually and in everything.

Now, people sometimes confuse giving thanks *in* everything with giving thanks *for* everything. There's a difference. You may be going through a difficult time right now, and the sorrow and pain you feel are real. Scripture tells you and me to give thanks in everything because we know that God can and will use it for good when we are called according to His purpose (Romans 8:28). You don't have to thank Him for that accident, bad diagnosis, or relational loss. But you do need to thank Him *in* it. Why? Because this demonstrates a heart of trust, and it lets both God and yourself know where your faith lies.

Keep in mind that you can never say thanks *for* some situations in life because that wouldn't make sense. If something is not good, it is not sourced in God. Yet whatever situation you find yourself in—good, bad, or ugly—you can give thanks *in* it because as a believer in Jesus Christ, you know that absolutely everything that happens to you passes through the fingers of God before it reaches you. And you can know that if it passed through God's fingers, He allowed it for a reason and a purpose.

Always view your pain through the lens of purpose. God has a way of turning a mess into a miracle when we approach that mess with the right heart attitude. God places everything you face in His cosmic blender in order to take you straight to the destiny He has prepared for you. Let the difficulties strengthen you and create in you a compassionate and humble heart. Let them motivate you to make His name great. Let the devil know through the fulfillment of your life's purpose that he picked the wrong person to mess with. Make him regret ever coming at you!

All things work together for good when you love God and walk in His purpose. God is creating good things in your life, and even though it doesn't always make sense, He will use every circumstance for good when you let Him. He can take nothing and make something out of it.

Your problems will be used by God. Your pain will be used by God. Your disappointments will be used by God. Your singlehood will be used by God. Your loneliness will be used by God. Your relational issues will be used by God. That doctor's analysis will be used by God. Let Him use these things by giving your lips to the surrender of thanks.

Now, I'm not saying to live in denial. If something fell on your big toe, it would hurt. Don't deny the pain. If your husband left you, that hurts. If you are tired of being single, that hurts. If you are broke, that hurts. That's real. Yet in the midst of the loss and confusion, understand that God is greater than all those things and more, and you can trust Him by giving thanks. You can trust Him to turn it around, to create your comeback, to bless you once again.

No matter what is wrong in your life, there is always something for which to give thanks.

How does God know you trust Him? Because you are thankful to Him *in* something even though you are not thankful *for* it. No matter what is wrong in your life, there is always something for which to give thanks.

Don't deny what is wrong, but don't forget to find a reason to give thanks. Be like the Puritan who had only bread and water but shouted out, "Bread, water, and Jesus too! Thank You!" If you don't have shoes, thank God for your feet. If you don't own a house, thank God for a roof over your head. If you don't have the dream job you want, thank God that you're working. In every situation, rather than complain, give thanks. Don't act as if God hasn't done anything.

If anyone had the right to complain, it was Joseph. He was sold into slavery, misjudged, mistreated, and thrown in jail for 13 years. But he is the one who said in Genesis 50:20, "You planned evil against me; God planned it for good to bring about the present result—the survival of many people." God meant it for good. When is your change going to come? I don't have the slightest idea. But I *do* know God's promise—if you will give thanks in everything, He will work it all out for good.

On top of that, you will also get peace. In Philippians 4:6-7 we read, "Don't worry about anything, but in everything, through prayer and petition with thanksgiving, let your requests be made known to God. And the peace of God, which surpasses every thought, will guard your hearts and minds in Christ Jesus."

Peace is a rare commodity these days. But it is yours for free when you choose to use your thoughts, lips, and words to give thanks.

Part 2

the perils of the tongue

Judgment in Your Jaws

During a routine medical examination, your family physician is likely to ask you to open your mouth, stick out your tongue, and say "aah." When she asks you to open your mouth and stick out your tongue, she is not merely looking for something wrong in your mouth. Rather, she understands that the condition of your mouth can indicate problems that go much deeper.

She looks in your mouth because it can sometimes indicate an infection elsewhere. It can sometimes indicate disease. Often it will indicate certain vitamin deficiencies. Simply by looking in your mouth, your doctor can determine whether something is wrong with you on a much deeper level.

Similarly, what comes out of your mouth matters much more than you think. What you say can reveal a deeper heart issue of sin that is infecting your life, decisions, and relationships. That's why this subject is so critical for the body of Christ to examine. Our mouths make a far greater difference and reveal a lot more than most of us realize.

In Matthew 12, we see Jesus performing some marvelous miracles. He has been blowing people's minds with what He is doing. In verses 22-23, He does a miracle. We read, "A demon-possessed man who was blind and unable to speak was brought to Him. He healed him, so that the man could both speak and see. And all the crowds were astounded." Jesus not only cast out the demons but also healed the man who had been unable to speak and see. Jesus healed his mouth.

The Pharisees didn't care for that sign of power so much, so they said, "The man drives out demons only by Beelzebul, the ruler of the demons" (verse 24). They accused Jesus of gaining His power to drive out demons from the devil himself. Christ's response to their accusation is packed with a much deeper spiritual truth related to the spoken word, and it carries great weight for us today.

> Every kingdom divided against itself is headed for destruction, and no city or house divided against itself will stand. If Satan drives out Satan, he is divided against himself. How then will his kingdom stand? And if I drive out demons by Beelzebul, who is it your sons drive them out by? For this reason they will be your judges. If I drive out demons by the Spirit of God, then the kingdom of God has come to you. How can someone enter a strong man's house and steal his possessions unless he first ties up the strong man? Then he can rob his house. Anyone who is not with Me is against Me, and anyone who does not gather with Me scatters. Because of this, I tell you, people will be forgiven every sin and blasphemy, but the blasphemy against the Spirit will not be forgiven. Whoever speaks a word against the Son of Man, it will be forgiven him. But whoever speaks against the Holy Spirit, it will not be forgiven him, either in this age or in the one to come (verses 25-32).

Jesus's response challenged the Pharisees' ability to think clearly. After all, how can a kingdom divided against itself stand? How could Satan hope to build his kingdom if Satan is casting out Satan? That didn't make any sense at all.

After providing this clarity, Jesus brings up a critical principle for the believer and nonbeliever's life, and that is the blasphemy against the Holy Spirit. He tells us that people who speak against Christ Himself can be forgiven. But people who speak against the Holy Spirit cannot be. This is because when people blaspheme the Holy Spirit, they reject the full light God has given them as an unambiguous statement that Jesus Christ is God. The Holy Spirit is the messenger of this truth to our own spirits. So when people speak against the Holy Spirit and reject Him, they remain in darkness. This is referring to unbelievers who reject the revealing illumination of the Spirit regarding the truth of God.

In WWII, an aircraft carrier in the Atlantic ocean had to turn off its lights so the enemy would not know its location. However, six planes had already taken off from the carrier, and with no lights on deck, the pilots could no longer see where to land. In desperation, they radioed the captain of the ship, pleading with him to turn the lights back on. But he was unable to do so without jeopardizing the entire ship. As a result, the six planes continued circling until they ran out of gas and ultimately ditched at sea because they could not land in darkness.

When unbelievers reject the revealing illumination of the Holy Spirit, only darkness can remain in them. To blaspheme the Holy Spirit, or to speak against Him, is to reject the Holy Spirit's revelation that Jesus is indeed the Christ, the Son of the Living God.

The Seriousness of Speech

Having said what He did about the eternal repercussions of

blaspheming the Holy Spirit, Jesus went on to another issue. He made a broader statement about speech in the next few verses.

> Either make the tree good and its fruit good, or make the tree bad and its fruit bad; for a tree is known by its fruit. Brood of vipers! How can you speak good things when you are evil? For the mouth speaks from the overflow of the heart. A good man produces good things from his storeroom of good, and an evil man produces evil things from his storeroom of evil. I tell you that on the day of judgment people will have to account for every careless word they speak. For by your words you will be acquitted, and by your words you will be condemned (Matthew 12:33-37).

Christ uses an illustration of a tree to reveal the source of our speech. He reminds us that a good tree will produce good fruit and a bad tree will produce bad fruit. If the fruit of a tree is good, you can assume the tree is also good. If the fruit of the tree is bad, the tree itself is bad.

Our words will always reflect what is already in our hearts.

Your heart is like the tree. Your words are like the fruit of that tree. Jesus is telling us that the fruit of our mouths—our words—will always reflect what is already in our hearts. "For the mouth speaks from the overflow of the heart" (verse 34). So if you have profane speech, it is because you have a profane heart. If you swear like a sailor, you have a sailor's heart. If you gossip, you have a gossip's heart. If you slander, you have a slanderer's heart.

Therefore, if you are trying to fix your mouth without changing your heart, you are setting yourself up for failure. It may work for a day or two, but the only sure way to fix your mouth is to address your heart. Otherwise, you are simply trying to manage a symptom rather than deal with the root problem.

Keep in mind that each of us has said things we regret. None of us speaks perfectly. Everyone reading this book has said things they wished they hadn't said or in a tone they wished they hadn't used. We all stumble in many ways. Christ is referring to that which fills the heart—what is being stored there. This is similar to a storage space you may have in your attic or in your garage. When the heart gets stored full of a particular emotion—perhaps fear, jealousy, or rage— it's eventually going to come out of the mouth. An overflow occurs simply because the mouth and the heart are connected.

Luke 6:45 says it this way: "A good man produces good out of the good storeroom of his heart. An evil man produces evil out of the evil storeroom, for his mouth speaks from the overflow of the heart." A more accurate titling of this book might then be *Watch Your Heart* because it's the heart that produces the language of the mouth.

In pastoral counseling, when I find mates who are mean with their mouths to each other on a regular basis (not a momentary slip), it is because they have mean hearts toward each other. The mouth is only articulating what the heart is declaring. In other words, the mouth is expressing what you cannot see, revealing that there is a disease inside. Matthew puts it this way:

> Don't you realize that whatever goes into the mouth passes
> into the stomach and is eliminated? But what comes out
> of the mouth comes from the heart, and this defiles a

man. For from the heart come evil thoughts, murders, adulteries, sexual immoralities, thefts, false testimonies, blasphemies. These are the things that defile a man, but eating with unwashed hands does not defile a man (Matthew 15:17-20).

The heart defiles you when its contents pass through your mouth. Selfishness, dishonesty, insecurity, envy…all these things proceed from the heart and out through the mouth. Before the words ever reach your tongue, they were formed in the recesses of your heart. The heart is the source of all speech.

Since the heart is the source of all speech, informing the lips of what to say, it's important to spend some time looking at the nature of the heart. Now, the Bible often uses physical terminology to reflect a spiritual truth or principle. In this case, when Scripture speaks of your heart, it is not talking about that mass of muscle pumping blood throughout your veins. Rather, it is referring to the contents of your soul.

As the physical heart exists to pump life throughout your physical body, your soul is your very life, the essence of who you are. When God created Adam, He breathed life into him, and Adam became "a living being," which literally means "a living soul" (Genesis 2:7). This gave Adam the capacity for fellowship with God, which was destroyed by sin.

The soul is comprised of three parts—your mind, your emotions, and your will. Your mind provides you with the capacity to think on the conscious and subconscious levels. Your emotions give you the ability to feel. And the will involves your capacity to make choices. These three intersect in the heart, which is the centerpiece of the soul. So when your mind, emotions, or will is filled with something that is negative or wrong, it will overflow to your mouth, affecting your speech.

When you came to Christ for the forgiveness of your sins, God saved you for heaven completely. But He saves you on earth progressively. It is possible to be once-and-for-all delivered for eternity but still be in the process of being delivered experientially in history.

This is because our souls are defective at birth due to inherited sin. They continue to be defective as we grow based on our experiences, the information we take in, and the joys and sorrows we experience. Every soul is distorted. Like a television unable to get good reception, the picture of our souls is fuzzy and distorted.

The problem is, most people settle for what I call "soul management." They try to make their souls better through commitments, seminars, New Year's resolutions, church attendance, service in ministries, and any number of other things. They are well meaning. But just like a television with poor reception, the soul cannot fix itself.

The soul has been damaged by this thing called sin. We have all been damaged—some of us worse than others. But God doesn't want us to focus on managing the distortion. Distortion will always be distortion, no matter how well it is managed. God offers something different—soul transformation. Jesus died on the cross not only to take your soul to heaven but also to deliver your soul in history.

But before deliverance can occur, a death must take place. Jesus said we must take up our cross daily and follow Him (Luke 9:23). In order for your soul to be alive, it must first die to itself. When you wake up each day, don't try to figure out how to control your thoughts, emotions, and will. Rather, surrender them to Christ, and if any part is not in alignment with God's rule in your life, let it die. As long as you try to keep your soul alive with its own will, it will continue to be distorted. The soul within you that needs to die is your self-life, your viewpoint on a matter...your will. This needs to be replaced with God's truth, His viewpoint, and a surrender and acceptance of His will.

Dying to Live

If you allow your viewpoint, emotions, and will to die, you then need to nourish the new life inside you in Christ. This new life first comes to you as a seed. When you trusted Jesus Christ as your Savior for the forgiveness of your sins, you received what the Bible calls an imperishable seed (1 Peter 1:23). This is your new nature. But too many believers haven't allowed that seed to germinate and grow and thrive. The reason why the seed is not working to bring about transformation is that the seed has not been allowed to expand.

The expansion of the seed affects the control of the soul. Even though you have the Spirit's life within you, if that seed is allowed to remain in seed form, the self-life will continue to rule. Unless a seed is planted and watered, it will not develop into any meaningful form of life. It contains life within it, but it won't be able to express that life and impact those around it.

A two-week old fetus in a mother's womb already has all the DNA it needs to reach its fullest potential of life. But that two-week old fetus doesn't express that life the same way a newborn baby does. The baby is more fully developed because the seed was able to grow.

James writes in the first chapter of his letter to tell us the secret of how this seed can expand. "My dearly loved brothers, understand this: Everyone must be quick to hear, slow to speak, and slow to anger" (1:19). Bear in mind that James is talking to Christians. He calls them "beloved brethren." So these verses apply only to those who have trusted Christ for their salvation. This is not a verse or spiritual truth about salvation, but rather about sanctification.

James clearly articulated in this passage that we are to be quick to hear, slow to speak, and slow to anger. The question you might be asking is, quick to hear what? The answer is, God's point of view on a matter.

The other question you might be asking is, slow to speak what? We are to be slow to speak our point of view on a matter. And when God's point of view differs from our point of view, we are to be slow to get angry about it.

However, we often flip it and do the opposite. We are quick to talk about our viewpoint, and we're slow to hear His point of view. This is why we go to everyone else first to find out what they think we should do before we go to God. But God says we should be quick to receive His point of view. We discover these truths in the next few verses: "Therefore, putting aside all filthiness and all that remains of wickedness, in humility receive the word implanted, which is able to save your souls" (James 1:21 NASB).

Now, remember, James is talking to people who are already saved. He just called them his "beloved brethren." Yet he is saying that their souls still need to be saved. This is because when you and I trusted Christ for the forgiveness of our sins, our souls were saved eternally, but our souls were not automatically saved (transformed) in history.

We are in the process of "being saved"—being transformed.

Jesus saved you for heaven in a flicker of time. But He saves you on earth progressively. First Corinthians 1:18 (NASB) tells us, "The word of the cross is foolishness to those who are perishing, but to us who are being saved it is the power of God." In that verse, the apostle Paul says we are in the process of "being saved"—being transformed.

In order for you to sanctify your soul (your heart) so that your mouth will reflect what is good, right, noble, and pure, you need to "receive the word implanted, which is able to save your souls." You do this first by removing anything that will interfere with the expansion of the implanted word. Just as a fertilized egg in a mother's womb requires nourishment to grow and develop into a newborn baby, the seed that has been implanted in you also requires nourishment. This nourishment is the Word of God. The Word of God must reach into the depth of your soul where the implanted word abides with the imperishable seed in order for that seed to expand and the new sanctified life to be expressed.

I've pastored a church for more than four decades, so I know first-hand that coming to church or reading your Bible is not the same thing as receiving the Word of God. In fact, it is possible to have the Word implanted but not to have received it. The word "receive" means to welcome. It means more than just simply hearing something, having something, or knowing something. It means to welcome it.

When you welcome someone who is standing at the door of your home, you invite that person in. That person is now inside your home. You didn't just stand at the door and say, "You are welcome." You ushered that person in—you experienced and lived out your welcome.

To receive the Word of God means it has to reach further than just your ears. Hearing a sermon on Sunday is good, but if it doesn't go further than your ears, it won't do the work of transforming your soul. If it doesn't go further than your immediate thoughts, it will not reach and change your heart.

A great deal of what happens in our lives is controlled by thoughts of which we are not even aware. These occur on the subconscious level. For example, try this experiment. Lift your right hand in the air. Great. Now, did you notice yourself thinking, "Muscles in my right arm, move and constrict so that the muscles in my right hand can be lifted"? I doubt it. None of us do. Our bodies regularly perform millions of functions that we do not knowingly think about, and yet without our subconscious thoughts, these functions would no longer occur. Similarly, you regularly perform routine actions without even thinking about them, such as brushing your teeth.

That is the level where the Word of God needs to be received—in the deepest core of your subconscious thoughts. And how does that happen? It's very similar to how you learn to ride a bike or brush your teeth so that eventually you can do it without even thinking about it. It is through repeated exposure to the same thing on a regular basis. We have a specific word for this when it comes to words and thoughts—meditation.

David writes about this in the book of Psalms when he says, "May the words of my mouth and the meditation of my heart be acceptable to You, LORD, my rock and my Redeemer" (Psalm 19:14).

The way to get our heart right is to get our meditations right.

The way to get our heart right is to get our meditations right. What is meditation? To meditate is to cogitate. It is to contemplate, to think about something repetitively, or to roll it around in your mind. Here's a crude example (but it works): Think about a cow. When a cow is hungry, it will go bite off some grass. Then it will chew it and chew it and chew it until the cow can swallow it. The problem is that the cow can't quite yet digest it, so it regurgitates the grass back into its mouth once again to continue chewing. That's why you can almost always catch a cow chewing something or having saliva running from its mouth. For cows, eating is a meditative process. They must chew on something over and over and over again.

One way to get God's Word into the deepest part of your spirit and soul—the part that will automatically affect your mind, your emotions, and your will because it is so ingrained in who you are—is to meditate on it. You must do more than simply read it once. Even more than memorize it. God's Word must be a continual and constant companion to your thoughts.

You might write God's Word on sticky notes and put them around your computer, in your car, or on your bathroom mirror. You might schedule a regular time each day to read and consider His Word, going back over it to make sure you are inputting it deeply. Your own approach will be based on your personality and lifestyle, so it may differ from mine or anyone else's. But the point is, however we do it, we must intentionally listen to, think on, read, and meditate on God's Word—His truths and principles. That includes listening to and reflecting on Scripture and sermons on a regular basis, not just on Sundays. Of course, that's easier than ever now with so many Internet tools at our disposal.

Have you noticed that Jesus often said, "He who has ears to hear, let him hear" (Matthew 11:15 NASB)? He's not talking about simply hearing what was spoken. Or about reading it in a book. Or reading it in your Bible. Jesus is saying to hear it in such a manner that you receive it. Receive the Word so that it can penetrate to the level of the division of soul and spirit (Hebrews 4:12). That requires thoughtful contemplation and meditation.

As the seed expands in your soul, it will begin to dominate your thoughts, feelings, and will so that what comes out of your mouth will reflect the viewpoint of God.

But in order to get to that point, you need to receive the Word implanted at a level where it is able to judge the thoughts and intentions of your heart (Hebrews 4:12 NASB). Remember—be quick to hear. Hear what? God's viewpoint on a matter. Be slow to speak. Speak what? Your viewpoint on a matter. And be slow to anger when His viewpoint is different from yours, your parents', your friends', and your coworkers'.

We've been referencing Hebrews 4:12, where the writer illustrates the word of God as a two-edged sword. It has two parts. It is both destructive and constructive. Anyone who has remodeled a house can understand this. In order to build up something new when you remodel a house, you must first tear something down. The Word of God also tears stuff down in order to make room for new life.

To transform your soul, you have to receive God's viewpoint, taking His Word into your spirit. And to attempt to fix the mouth without changing the soul (the heart) will not fix anything at all.

When you squeeze an orange, you are going to get orange juice. When you squeeze a lemon, you'll make lemonade. Whatever exists within your soul, or your heart, will be what routinely overflows through your mouth. That is why it says in Proverbs, "A wise heart instructs its mouth and increases learning with its speech" (16:23). And elsewhere in Proverbs, "Guard your heart above all else, for it is the source of life" (4:23).

Survey Your Speech

After talking about the source of our speech, which is the soul (the heart), Jesus goes on to say, "I tell you that on the day of judgment people will have to account for every careless word they speak. For by your words you will be acquitted, and by your words you will be condemned" (Matthew 12:36-37). Essentially, God has put a wiretap on your mouth and is listening to every word you say. In addition, every careless word is being noted. Every useless, evil, unrighteous, and untrue word will be accounted for on the day of judgment. That's enough to make me want to not say much of anything at all!

God has put a wiretap on your mouth and
is listening to every word you say.

When you stand before the judgment seat of Christ to gain or lose rewards, your words will either work for you (you will be acquitted) or against you (you will be condemned). That judgment day is not the judgment that determines your eternal salvation. This is a separate judgment, when God determines the rewards and responsibilities He will give you or take from you in heaven.

See, we won't all be on the same level in heaven. We are not all equal there. Your words and your works on earth will determine your experience of heaven. Wouldn't it be terrible to try so hard your whole life to live an exemplary Christian life, only to get to heaven and discover that your words have condemned you and removed a large portion of the reward you had earned? That's the power of your words. That right there ought to encourage you to watch your mouth and guard it closely—starting right now.

God is listening to every word, and that includes the words you say under your breath about your boss or family member. It includes the times you speak unkindly when you get angry. It includes the lies, arrogance, envy, and put-downs.

Friend, this truth ought to be life-changing. When eternal rewards are attached to your words, it doesn't seem worth it to speak so many negative things anymore, does it? But remember, in order to truly watch your mouth, you will have to watch your heart. You will have to intentionally and deliberately go about receiving the implanted Word, which will transform your soul. Make Psalm 19:14 your daily prayer: "May the words of my mouth and the meditation of my heart be acceptable to You, LORD, my rock and my Redeemer."

10

Evil in Your Esophagus

A woman went to the doctor one day because she was very sick. She had been bitten by an animal some time before, so the doctor took a look at her bite. He also ran some lab work, and it revealed that this woman had rabies—in an advanced, incurable stage.

The doctor told the woman, "I'm sorry, ma'am, but it doesn't look good."

The woman looked at the doctor and asked him for a piece of paper and a pen. The doctor was a little confused by her request, but he found what she needed and gave them to her. Once she received the paper and pen, the woman began to write down some names.

The doctor asked, "Are you writing down the names of the people you want to put in your will?"

The woman replied, "Oh no, doctor, not at all. I'm writing down the names of the people I want to bite."

Friend, one of the ways people demonstrate how sick they are is with their mouths. In our mouths are physical germs as well as spiritual germs. When we bite others with our words, we cause them to be sick. Our speech can damage others.

Perhaps you've experienced this firsthand. You've said something
in a moment of pain, hurt, or anger, and you noticed it's damaging
effect on another person. They may have become sad or angry, or they
may have even tried to hurt themselves. Or maybe you've been on the
receiving end of rabid language—toxic speech that just wouldn't leave
your system. It made your blood curdle and your stomach churn. Our
mouths are dangerous on many levels. As we saw in the introduc-
tion, they can actually speak death into our own lives and situations
as well as into others'.

No one intentionally sets out to ruin their relationships, their
career, or any other part of their life. But too often this happens as
a result of being unaware of the corrupting influence of our words
and the damage they can cause. That's why I'm going to take the next
three chapters to look at specific and common ways that happens.

How can you tell when your talk is not what it ought to be?

Let's start by asking this practical question: How can you tell when
your talk is not what it ought to be? One identifying factor is its effect
on other people. Does what you say pull people down or build them
up? Do the words from your mouth inspire or destroy? After people
spend time with you, do they walk away with a smile on their face and
pep in their step, or do they walk away with their head hung down,
their energy drained, and the light lost from their eyes?

Many of us don't realize the negative effect our words have on
other people. At work, whenever someone has an idea or shares a
vision, some people respond with ten reasons why it could never

work. Others always look tired, and their words reflect a spirit of apathy or criticism. Still others always seem to focus attention on themselves regardless of the topic of conversation. In each case, a roomful of people can be adversely affected by one person's inappropriate words.

Gossip

Words matter—they can give us enthusiasm or deplete it. They can give us hope or crush it. They can protect our reputations or destroy them. Proverbs 20:19 says, "The one who reveals secrets is a constant gossip; avoid someone with a big mouth." You can't get any more straightforward than that! The Bible is replete with pearls of wisdom, and that one is among the best. Do you want to avoid problems in your life, pain in your heart, and unnecessary issues? One way to do that is to avoid people who have big mouths.

Proverbs tells us elsewhere what kind of people we should seek out for our relationships: "A gossip goes around revealing a secret, but a trustworthy person keeps a confidence" (Proverbs 11:13). A gossip is a revealer of secrets. A trustworthy person is a protector of privacy. Never trust a talebearer, but rather, surround yourself with those who neither tell tales nor repeat a bad report. If a friend starts a conversation by saying, "You need to pray for so-and-so because..." put your alert up. If the thing that they share next would best be kept private, you can be sure this same friend will most likely be willing to share with others anything you say.

Or if you are that person who feels the need to go around and spread everyone's business (disguised of course as a prayer request), understand that Scripture is warning people to stay away from you. That's not a good position to be in as a follower of Christ. Yes, Jesus loves you, but He may not want His other children to spend much time talking with you—not until you learn to bridle your tongue.

Proverbs 18:8 puts it this way: "A gossip's words are like choice food that goes down to one's innermost being." They are sweet to the taste and juicy with each bite. That's why you'll hear someone say when they listen to a piece of gossip, "Oh, that's juicy...that's really juicy." They talk about the words as if they were talking about food because the Bible itself compares gossiping to eating. We chew each morsel, swallow it, and digest it, allowing it to shape our thoughts, reactions, and responses to the subject or person it was about.

The apostle Paul knew the danger of gossip, and it disturbed him greatly. So much so that he didn't even want to go visit those he loved dearly at the church he started in Corinth. He was afraid of what he would find when he arrived because he knew their propensity toward gossip and other verbal sins. He wrote, "I fear that perhaps when I come I will not find you to be what I want...there may be quarreling, jealousy, outbursts of anger, selfish ambitions, slander, gossip, arrogance, and disorder" (2 Corinthians 12:20). Paul knew the danger of the mouth and the damage it can do, and it grieved him to realize these verbal sins were common in a church he had begun.

We sadden God when we speak unholy
language about someone else.

Imagine how it grieves the heart of God when He hears us hurting others He made in His own image and loved enough to die for. We sometimes forget that we sadden God when we speak unholy language about someone else. We forget that the Lord loves this person as much as He loves us, and hurting them with our words hurts God too.

Unholy speech erects a barrier in our personal, intimate relationship with God and also erects a barrier between people on earth. Proverbs 16:28 tells us, "A contrary man spreads conflict, and a gossip separates close friends." Gossip is a surefire way to destroy relationships. And it is one of the deadliest tools the enemy uses. Keep in mind that a gossip never seeks to help or to heal—even if their words are couched in concern. A gossip enjoys disseminating information that paints someone else in a bad light—or paints the gossiper in a greater light for being privy to something most people are not.

This reminds me of the story of the four preachers who went on a little retreat and decided they would have a time of joint confession. The preachers had set aside this time in order to talk about their own struggles, sins, and situations. The first preacher began by saying, "Well, I've struggled with gambling over the years. In fact, I gamble online when the family isn't home." The rest of the preachers nodded their heads and agreed they would pray with him.

After him, the second preacher opened up and said, "I can't control my temper. If my kids do the slightest things to annoy me, I go off on them because I feel mad." The preachers again said they would pray for him and seek to hold him accountable so that his anger wouldn't adversely affect his home.

The preachers were really feeling comfortable with each other by this point, so the third preacher opened up that he struggled with pornography. In fact, he went even further and asked the other preachers to help him stop his addiction. They all agreed that they would be there for him, and this third preacher seemed to relax in that reality.

That is, until the fourth preacher spoke up. It was his time to share his vice with the group, but he told the other preachers he didn't want to. They asked him why, and he responded that they probably didn't know about his sin. But they continued to encourage him to open up, so he decided he would go ahead and reveal his issue. "Well," the fourth man said, "my struggle has always been with gossip."

The rest of the group were stunned, the blood draining from their faces.

Be careful what you say because words can grow legs.

One of the reasons why people gossip, and one reason why you may find yourself gossiping, has to do with having too much time on your hands. The Bible calls it being idle. Timothy writes, "They also learn to be idle, going from house to house; they are not only idle, but are also gossips and busybodies, saying things they shouldn't say" (1 Timothy 5:13). The telephone becomes a friend of someone who is idle—and not a good friend at all. Texting becomes a way of filling time. Gossip becomes a distraction from the duties of life—our own little soap opera or reality-TV show. We don't even have to reach for the remote, because the entertainment comes right out of our own mouths these days.

But gossip is not entertainment to God. In fact, in Romans 1:26-32, God puts gossip side by side with the sins of homosexuality, murder, and malice. So before you go cherry-picking sins and pointing fingers at others, be sure to read how God lines them up. You might be surprised and choose to watch your mouth.

Slander

Slander is gossip's twin. To slander is to speak evil of another in order to defame them. Gossip is talking about someone's actions (what they did), but slander is talking about someone's character (who they are). When you defame someone, damaging their reputation, your words can have lasting repercussions. People may gossip to pass the time or feel better about themselves, but to slander is to speak evil with the intent to hurt. Gossip may come as a whisper, but slander is spoken openly. Slander seeks to destroy.

Why is slander so serious for a believer? Psalm 15 asks, "LORD, who can dwell in Your tent? Who can live on Your holy mountain?" Then David answers his own question: "The one who lives honestly, practices righteousness, and acknowledges the truth in his heart—who does not slander with his tongue, who does not harm his friend or discredit his neighbor" (verses 1-3).

Slander is serious business because it disqualifies you from experiencing the manifest presence of God in your life. It removes you from His dwelling place. It separates you from fellowship with the Creator of the universe and the Ruler over all. When you look at slander that way, is it even worth it? You're not only hurting another person—you're hurting yourself even more.

The Bible tells us that when you slander, you damage not only your relationship with God but also your relationships in the body of Christ. Paul says, "I wrote to you not to associate with any so-called brother if he is an immoral person…or a reviler…not even to eat with such a one" (1 Corinthians 5:11 NASB).

A slanderer is a fool. Those aren't my words, they are God's. "He who conceals hatred has lying lips, and he who spreads slander is a fool" (Proverbs 10:18 NASB).

Slanderers have one basic motivation. They are insecure people who seek to raise their own status by demeaning someone else. In other words, if a slanderer can push you down, he can lift himself up—at least that's how he sees things. John called out someone like this in his writings: "I wrote something to the church; but Diotrephes, who loves to be first among them, does not accept what we say" (3 John 9). Apparently Diotrephes wanted to have top billing among the brethren, so he wouldn't allow others to have their own thoughts or their own insights. He made it difficult for anyone else to shine. One way that is done is through slander.

Now, before I step on too many toes, I want to clarify that a slanderer is not someone who has slipped up here or there or has tripped over his or her own tongue. Slanderers are people who do this on a regular basis or anytime they need a way to lift themselves up. This is the way they roll—it's their MO.

Slander is an enormous sign of immaturity.

Slander is an enormous sign of immaturity because it broadcasts the slanderer's deep lack of faith in God. Rather than trusting God to ordain their steps or open up doors of promotion, they take matters into their own hands. People often use gossip and slander in the workforce to maneuver their way up the ladder.

God can overrule bosses, supervisors, and managers. He can make connections you never thought possible. He can get you where you need to go, so you never need to put someone else down to lift yourself up. Not in God's kingdom economy. In fact, when you put someone else down, you are actually putting yourself down. James writes, "God resists the proud, but gives grace to the humble" (James 4:6).

In fact, God tells us that when we see our brother or sister stumbling, rather than slandering them or gossiping about it, we are to cover them and help turn them back to the right path. We read, "My brothers, if any among you strays from the truth, and someone turns him back, let him know that whoever turns a sinner from the error of his way will save his life from death and cover a multitude of sins" (James 5:19-20).

Now, God never tells us to excuse sin. He doesn't ask us to pretend that sin is not sin. Rather, He says our responsibility in His family is to turn our brother or sister right when they have gone left. Our goal is to get them moving once again in the right direction. "Brothers, if someone is caught in any wrongdoing, you who are spiritual should restore such a person with a gentle spirit, watching out for yourselves so you also won't be tempted" (Galatians 6:1).

This is what happened in a story that is often not preached about but has a significant application for our lives. It is found in Genesis 9:20-28, where Noah planted a vineyard and did a little too much wine tasting. As a result, he wound up lying naked and uncovered in an inappropriate manner. When one of Noah's sons saw his father naked, he went out and slandered his father to his brothers. His two brothers, on the other hand, backed into the tent where their father lay, and they covered him.

God's response to this ought to be a wake-up call, changing the way we respond to our brothers and sisters who are struggling. God was so angry at the brother who had slandered his father, He cursed that brother's first son, Canaan. Because of the shame this son had brought to his dad, God said his own sons would bring him shame as well.

God's actions did not justify Noah's sin. The other two brothers' actions—averting their eyes and covering their father—didn't condone it. Rather, these righteous actions provided the opportunity for Noah's dignity to be restored. Dignity is important because we are all made in the image of God.

This reminds me of a time when I was still living at home and my brother did something entirely wrong. Being the self-appointed police in the life of my siblings, I told my dad, and he let my brother have it. My brother got what is called a "session." Yet when my brother's session was done, my dad called me in for mine as well. I was in complete shock and disbelief!

"What?" I asked.

"You heard me. It's your turn," my dad replied.

I asked my dad why, and he responded, "You could have helped your brother realize what he was doing wrong and stop it on his own. If your motivation had been love for your brother, that's what you would have done. Instead, you just wanted him to get in trouble. So because of that, you're in trouble too."

See, in a family, the goal is not to hurt each other, but rather to help each other become as strong and mature as possible. The same is true in the family of God.

Gossip and slander bring damage not only to the person involved but also to the other people around the situation. Neither of these should happen in the body of Christ. That's madness. In Proverbs we read, "Like a madman who throws flaming darts and deadly arrows, so is the man who deceives his neighbor and says, 'I was only joking!'" (26:18-19). As we see from this verse, people will sometimes cradle a lie in a joke and then follow it up with, "I'm just kidding," or "I'm just sayin'." Whether it comes as a full-on attack or a subtle deception, it's a lie to God, and His opinion matters most. God says don't do it at all.

Rather, God desires for us to create an environment that helps others rather than hurting them. An atmosphere of trust that provides healing, not harming. When we honor the Lord with our lips and refrain from gossip and slander, we invite Him to show up in our midst and do great things through our lives.

Words are powerful. For good and for bad. And once spoken, they are difficult to retrieve. In fact, do me a favor now that this chapter is coming to a close. Will you go get your tube of toothpaste, or get it when you get home? Squeeze some of the toothpaste out of it.

Now put it back in.

Just as it is impossible to do that, you likewise cannot retrieve your words or their impact once you have spoken them.

11

Satan in Your Speech

A man was pulling out of a parking space when he accidentally hit another man's parked car. The offender got out of his car and began to write a note. The note said, "Everybody looking at me right now thinks I'm leaving my name, address, and phone number. I am not. Good luck." It looked like the man was doing the right thing, but he was not.

Then there was the man who went fishing but had a very bad day. He caught nothing. On his way home he stopped by the grocery store and told the person behind the meat counter, "Give me ten of your largest fish so I can tell my wife I caught them." He reconfigured life's circumstances so he could say one thing while meaning another.

Or the boy who seemed to be lost. People were feeling sorry for him, so they began to give him a little money to buy food. Finally, someone touched him on the shoulder and said, "I think I see your mother over there."

"Shhh," he replied. "I see her too, but I don't need to find her right now."

Deception

These three stories are examples of deception—one of the ways Satan worms his way into your speech. Deception is tricking people with your speech in order to bring a greater benefit to you. It's a form of lying, but it is sprinkled with the sauce of sneaking, tricking, or exaggerating.

We've all deceived people at some time. Perhaps we described a past event as bigger and more grand than it actually was. Or we downplayed something we did wrong because we didn't want to own up to it. It could be something as simple as telling your wife you had only a bite of that doughnut, knowing full well that bite equaled two-thirds of the whole thing.

Deception is difficult for listeners to discern, and it can be even more difficult for the speaker to stop. This reminds me of the story of the farmer whose watermelons were being stolen by some neighborhood boys. The farmer thought long and hard about how to stop these boys from taking his watermelons. Finally he decided to put up a sign in his patch that read, "One of these watermelons is poisonous!"

The farmer congratulated himself because he thought that was a brilliant idea—that is, until he went to his watermelon patch the next day and saw that someone had taken a pen to his sign. The word "one" was crossed out, and over it was written the word "two." The farmer had no choice but to forfeit his whole crop—all because he tried to deceive these boys. Deception can come back to bite you.

In 1 Peter 3:10 we find a verse that speaks directly to this malady of the mouth. "The one who wants to love life and to see good days must keep his tongue from evil and his lips from speaking deceit." Peter is saying that your well-being is connected to how you use your tongue, whether deceptively or honestly. If you want to see good days in your life, then watch your mouth. Model your words after God, not Satan. After all, Satan is known as "the father of lies" (John 8:44 NASB).

We see Satan playing out his strategy of deception in the Garden of Eden. Sin entered the universe on the crafty words of a snake. Eve was duped into eating from the tree of the knowledge of good and evil. She got tricked. She was played.

So powerful is the deceptive nature of the devil that one-third of all the angels followed him out of heaven when he tried to usurp the throne of God, their Creator. The fallen angel must have taken notes in heaven while he was there, because as we've seen, "Satan disguises himself as an angel of light" (2 Corinthians 11:14) in order to deceive. He comes looking like a friend in order to be a more effective enemy. And one of his greatest strategies is to get you to use deception yourself. That way you do the work for him. When you or I deceive others, we unintentionally join the devil. We are engaging in the spiritual practices of hell.

Only truth can bring freedom.

As a result, we are holding our own dreams, wants, and relationships hostage because only truth can bring freedom (John 8:32). When the devil is able to deceive you, he owns you. You may know what it is like to be owned by a lie—to have believed something about yourself that you now know is not true. It affected your thoughts, decisions, your conversations, and your relationships.

Far too many people believe they are not good enough or talented enough to do great things for God, so they don't even try. They are being held hostage by this deception, but the apostle Paul demonstrates the truth: "I am able to do all things through Him who strengthens me" (Philippians 4:13).

Deception is tricky to pick up on because it usually includes a little bit of truth wrapped in a lie. Satan combined a morsel of truth with a helping of lies when he served Eve an appetizer of deception. What Satan did with Eve in the garden, he seeks to do with us every day. He tries to get us to remove our focus from the goodness of God and all the trees we can freely eat from. He does this because he knows that the only way he can defeat us is through deception. Truth exists within the goodness of God, and wherever the truth of God is present, Satan's ability to deceive is diminished.

Satan's tricks of deception are so crafty, you cannot fight him with your own strength, your own methods, or your own thoughts. Only God's Word—His truth—can trump Satan. You can't. I can't. Satan has constitutional superiority over every man and woman because he is a spirit being. He is not bound by the limitations of flesh and blood. Therefore, you cannot compete with his ability to deceive. He is the master chameleon.

The devil's ultimate purpose is to deceive the entire world and lead us away from God's truth. To understand how he does this, consider the way a fisherman sets out to catch a fish. If a fisherman were to put a hook in the water all by itself, he would be waiting there a long time before anything bit his hook. In fact, it's doubtful that anything ever would. Instead, the fisherman puts a worm on the hook to deceive a fish into thinking it's getting an easy snack.

Satan doesn't simply throw hooks out to us either. He doesn't advertise on the liquor bottle, "Drink me and get drunk, become addicted to drugs or alcohol, lose your family, lead your kids into alcoholism, and throw away your future." Rather, Satan is a salesman. He uses the "foot in the door" technique to wiggle his way far enough into your mind to make it difficult for you to push him back out.

Satan tries to get you to let him into your life little by little. First, it's just a foot in the door—maybe a movie you shouldn't have watched, a conversation you shouldn't have had, or a relationship you shouldn't have pursued. At first, it seems harmless. But as Satan makes his way in, it becomes easier to buy what he is selling.

Whatever controls your mind controls your
mouth and thus controls your actions.

The primary way Satan does this is by planting an illegitimate or sinful idea in our minds. This is what he did with David. "Satan stood up against Israel and incited David to count the people of Israel" (1 Chronicles 21:1). David got the idea that he didn't need God at that point and that he was able to take care of his army himself. As a result, he disobeyed God's instructions, and as a result 70,000 people lost their lives.

Whatever controls your mind controls your mouth and thus controls your actions.

Why do people listen to the devil's lies, whether bold or subtle, rather than rest in God's promises? One main reason is that people don't know God's Word well enough to tell the difference between the truth and a lie. Daily Bible study—meditating on and memorizing God's Word—can help you know God's truth and apply it to your life. When you do that, you will be ready for Satan's lies when he comes against you. Ephesians 6:17 tells us to arm ourselves for spiritual battle with the sword of the Spirit, which is the word of God.

Jesus was our example during His temptation in the wilderness. He spoke the Word of God right back to the perverter of truth, and the Word carried Him to victory. That's why the greatest, most effective approach you can take to overcome Satan's deception in your own life and your own deceptive speech is to know, believe, and speak God's Word. When you believe God's Word in your heart and speak it with your mouth, God stands behind you and makes it real in your life. God manifests His power when you *use* His Word, not when you merely *know* it. You need to speak it when Satan knocks on your door or when you feel tempted to be deceptive yourself. Confess what God says to be true, and Satan will flee. Confessing the Word means to say the same thing God says and then to apply it personally to yourself.

The reason God's Word works so well is that it is alive and powerful (Hebrews 4:12). It is a two-edged sword. Since all Scripture is God-breathed (2 Timothy 3:16), it bears God's authority when utilized. This also makes it comprehensive in its impact (verse 17). God's Word is to be in our mouths at all times because what He says is settled in heaven. It is done. It is over. Therefore His Word is effective in whatever it seeks to accomplish (Psalm 119:89; Isaiah 55:11; 1 Thessalonians 2:13).

God wants us not only to read, study, and memorize His Word, but also to obediently and openly declare what it says (Joel 3:10; Hebrews 13:5-6). Practically this means you must find out what God says about a matter in Scripture and then declare it to be true—to yourself, to Satan, and to the situation that needs to hear it.

The more of the truth you know, the freer you will become.

The way to defeat deception in your own mouth, in others' words, and in the enemy's lies is through the truth. The more of the truth you know, the freer you will become. And it will be easier for you to recognize deception when it is coming at you or when you yourself are speaking. When the truth is deep within your soul, it will convict you and establish itself as a guard over your mouth. Truth is essential if you want to grow stronger, thrive, and stay on the path God has for you.

In Judges 16 we find the well-known story of Samson and Delilah—a perfect example of what can result from deception. Delilah was on a mission to discover what made Samson so strong, so she intentionally deceived him to get to his secret. Even worse, Samson was aware of her deception, and yet he chose to respond with deception of his own. We read, "Delilah said to Samson, 'Behold, you have deceived me and told me lies; now please tell me how you may be bound'" (verse 10 NASB).

A web of lies was being strung on both sides. Delilah wasn't revealing her true intention of selling Samson out. Samson was avoiding a truthful answer to her questions.

Deception creates chaos and eventually leads to ruin. When Samson eventually gave in, he was overcome by the enemy and taken down. By allowing himself to remain in a deceptive relationship, Samson not only lost his strength—he lost his future.

Friend, deception can cost you more than you even realize. That's why it is so critical to watch your mouth—and when you recognize deception coming from the mouths of those around you, to address it or move on when possible. Deception is not a game to play—it's the primary tool of the enemy.

Flattery

Clearly associated with deception is the use of flattery. Flattery is a chocolate-covered lie. It's a strawberry lie dipped in a sweet covering. Flattery offers up sweet words, yet they come laced with the poison of manipulation. The purpose of flattery is always to gain favor. It is not a compliment given for the sake of expressing true appreciation. Rather, it is an intentional use of words to gain a position of advantage. Some people use flattery so often, they don't even notice they are doing it. They butter people up so they can use them for their own purposes. After all, most of us will respond to flattery. Who doesn't enjoy hearing compliments of how great we look, how well we do something, and the like?

Scripture has harsh words to say about the use of flattery. Jude writes about flattery in relation to false teachers when he says, "These are grumblers, finding fault, following after their own lusts; they speak arrogantly, flattering people for the sake of gaining an advantage" (Jude 16 NASB). Psalm 12 tells us that flatterers will be judged in the strictest of ways: "May the Lord cut off all flattering lips, the tongue that speaks great things" (Psalm 12:3 NASB). The Bible is letting us know that flattery is so damaging, manipulating, deceptive, and wrong that God would rather see the tongue removed altogether than allow it to continue.

Flattery is an insincere compliment designed to deceive the intended hearer or hearers in order to gain control over them. Flattery looks like a friend the same way a wolf looks like a dog. It may appear fluffy and cute, but it will rip you to shreds if you get close enough. It is Judas approaching Jesus with a kiss, a sign of affection, at the very moment of humanity's greatest betrayal. Judas distorted the purity of love and kindness in order to accomplish evil. In the book of Job we read, "Let me now be partial to no one, nor flatter any man" (Job 32:21-22 NASB). In other words, Job was stating he would be honest with all. God honors honesty and lips that speak the truth.

God detests deception and hates flattery so much that He condemns them: "Such men are slaves, not of our Lord Christ but of their own appetites; and by their smooth and flattering speech they deceive the hearts of the unsuspecting" (Romans 16:18).

Is God making a mountain out of a molehill by speaking in

the Bible so harshly against flattery? After all, who doesn't love a compliment?

Flattery is the most cunning form of deception
and manipulation. It is sheer evil.

The problem is that flattery is not just a compliment. Compliments are great. Flattery is the use of smooth language with the intent to gain an advantage over someone else's thoughts and actions. It is the most cunning form of deception and manipulation. It is sheer evil, and it reveals a heart that does not trust in God's power to guide and direct our paths and work in our relationships. It reveals a lack of faith. David's prayer in Psalm 51:10 ought to be our own each and every day: "Create in me a clean heart, O God." A clean heart cannot flatter because light drives out darkness, and purity removes deception.

Bearing False Witness

Another form of deception is closely related to gossip, slander, and flattery—bearing false witness. Bearing false witness means to intentionally deceive by giving false information to the hurt and harm of others. Many people who believe lying is a sin also believe it is a very present help in the time of trouble.

We lie for a lot of reasons. To impress people, to trick people, to get revenge, to make a profit, to hurt others, to escape consequences, and so on. It is often camouflaged with flattery (1 Thessalonians 2:5) and with jokes (Proverbs 26:16-28).

The ninth commandment strictly prohibits the bearing of false witness (Exodus 20:16). The concept was related to a court of law where a false witness received the same judgment he intended for the person he lied about (Deuteronomy 19:16-21).

God allows for this type of deception in only one situation—when not to do so would result in committing or participating in a greater sin, such as murder. For example, the midwives in Egypt deceived Pharaoh about the birth of Hebrew babies in order to save the babies' lives (Exodus 1:15-21), and Rahab lied about hiding the Jewish spies so they wouldn't be captured (Joshua 2:1-21).

God is a God of truth and commands us to be people of truth (1 John 1:5-10).

Jesus was the only preacher who didn't seem to mind making His congregations smaller with His sermons. He would have big crowds following Him, and then He would come up with a line like "No one can come to Me unless it is granted to him by the Father" (John 6:65). The next verse says many of His disciples turned back and no longer accompanied Him. Why? Because He never let the crowd control the truth.

Jesus never flattered others, nor did He seek it out. Likewise, out of His mouth came no manipulation, deception, or false witness. That's the same mouth that got a dead man up and out of a grave simply by saying His name. Do you want your lips to have the power to move mountains in your life and restore life to dead situations? Then let your lips be like Christ's in every way.

Dirt in Your Discourse

Most of us need mouthwash in the morning. You are a unique person if you do not need to use mouthwash to get rid of the germs and bacteria that collected overnight. In fact, many of us could stand to use mouthwash after lunch and dinner as well. That's why the business of selling breath mints and gum has become so successful. All these products have become normal and natural parts of our lives simply because fighting bad breath has become a normal and natural part of our lives. Mouthwash, breath mints, and chewing gum are designed to cleanse the mouth from the things that cause bad breath. They attack the source of bad breath so people won't mind being around us when we speak with them.

We are living in a day when people need some spiritual mouthwash because of the irreverence spewing out their mouths. This is a day of evil speech. Our culture has tossed off all restraint when it comes to the kind of language people use, how and when they use it, and with whom. We have hundreds of public school teachers and employees at the church where I pastor, and they tell me that elementary school kids are now resorting to cussing them out. When kids feel free to swear, what does that say about the atmosphere in which we are raising them?

Television, social media, and the Internet have become our children's parents. As a result, they are exposed to lewdness and irreverence on a constant basis. As is anyone who engages in those worlds. I remember when the classic film *Gone with the Wind* was still causing such a stir because it introduced a swear word at the close of the movie. Yet these days, you're hard pressed to find a film that isn't filled with coarse language. The shock value is gone from our consciences. Comedians understand that to make their jokes get a greater response, they need to use profanity and vulgarity. Somehow disrespect has become entertaining.

Each and every one of us has been affected by unwholesome talk at some point. We may work in an environment where that's the common language, or we may have even fallen into it ourselves. Too much of what we hear and what we say today is laced with a liberal dose of inappropriate talk.

When it comes to promoting reverence in our mouths, God doesn't mince words.

So many of the people who feel free to praise God on Sunday feel just as free to laugh at filth the rest of the week. Free speech has become more important than clean speech. Yet for Christians, God has something important to say on the dirt in our discourse. It is not a subject to take lightly. When it comes to promoting reverence in our mouths, God doesn't mince words.

In Ephesians 4:29 we read, "No foul language is to come from your mouth, but only what is good for building up someone in need, so that it gives grace to those who hear." Christians who are serious about their faith should not be known for the foul language coming from their mouths. That does not merely refer to swearing. In this passage, foul language is contrasted with words that build up people who are in need and that give grace to the listeners. Foul language tears people down or offends their ears.

Too many people today suffer from loose lips. Because of their frustration, boredom, or simple displeasure, they run their mouths unless someone sets up boundaries to stop them. We often call this "venting," but it's more like spewing. They are spewing the contents of their hearts because whatever is said reflects the heart. A profane or foulmouthed person has a profane heart.

Now, I'm not talking about the individual who occasionally has a slip of the tongue. I'm talking about people whose MO is to speak harshly and irreverently. This is bigger than speech. This is about people's hearts. People who feel comfortable entering others' personal space with uninvited foul language have a disrespectful heart. Their hearts are caught up in pride, because they assume that other person is not worth the effort it takes to watch their mouth.

Ephesians 5:4 tells us more about this. "Coarse and foolish talking or crude joking are not suitable, but rather giving thanks." Paul warns us against letting gutter speech become our normal speech. The world has lost its conscience and self-control, but we should not lose ours. You cannot help the fact that it's all around you—you can't control what other people are saying. But Paul makes the point of saying that no unwholesome talk should come out of your own mouth. You *can* control your mouth. You may not be able to stop other people from using foul language around you, but you can stop yourself from joining in.

We need to feel the way God feels about foul language. Otherwise, we'll think it's not so bad. It's too prevalent today to not get that impression.

One day a preacher's daughter stubbed her toe and immediately blurted out, "Darn!"

Now, saying "darn" is not that bad, but her father didn't want her to start in that direction, so he came up with an idea. He said, "Baby, I'll give you a quarter if you promise me you'll never say 'darn' again."

His daughter thought about his request and then replied, "Okay, Daddy. But I got a word worth a dollar too!"

It's amazing what you'll say if the money is right.

Yet God does not want you to say any of it. He doesn't want unwholesome speech to be a part of your vocabulary. This is because speech matters.

When you feel tempted to adopt the speech of the culture, remind yourself that you are called to be in the world but not of the world (John 17:16). Just as a boat floats on the water but will sink if it is filled with water, you can navigate through our culture but must not let it define you. When it comes to your mouth, you have a higher standard than the world does.

Taking the Lord's Name in Vain

One of the worst examples of the dirt in our discourse has to do with taking God's name in vain. God does not want His name to be used as a divine exclamation point (Matthew 5:33-37; James 5:12). Rather, He wants His name to be used only when it reflects the glory of His person (Psalm 29:1-2).

Exodus 20:7 puts this as one of only ten commandments God laid down when developing His relationship with the nation of Israel and ultimately with us. To take a name in vain means that it is said in emptiness, without worth, purpose, or value. That means more than just saying God's name as a cuss word. It includes belittling the honor of His name by blurting it out in connection with anything that is beneath Him. And what's even worse is to attach profanity to God's name. You have not only used His name void of its content but also ascribed content from the devil in connection with the Creator of all.

No one I know likes to hear his or her name put down, tossed under the bus, or dismissed. Why would God feel any less strongly about His own name? And yet people do that all the time to the God who created them, sustains them with life, and loved them enough to send His only Son to die for their sins. Whenever God's name is used outside the context of what is true, it is void of the reality of who He is. God's name is not common, and He does not want it to be treated commonly. It's holy, and therefore it should be set apart in its use.

If God can't sign off on it, don't attach His name to it. That's spiritual forgery.

Unfortunately today, God's name gets forged on a lot of things He never signed off on. Whenever we use His name apart from the revelation of His nature and His character, we commit a forgery. If God can't sign off on it, don't attach His name to it. That's spiritual forgery.

We often do this when we want to justify a decision we are making. Many people will say, "God told me to do this." Or we do it when we want to say something to someone else that may not go over too well. We may begin by saying, "God put it on my heart to share this with you." God does guide, lead, direct, and instruct, but we illegitimately attribute to Him far too much of what we want to do, simply because His names bears a weight greater than our own. Yet when we do that, we are using God's name in vain.

Yes, it makes it sound more official when you attach God's name to whatever plans or thoughts you have. But if God didn't make it plain with you, and you just want to do it, be careful of adding His stamp of approval to what is solely yours to own. That's using God's name to promote yourself, and He doesn't take lightly to it. Most of us in the body of Christ could stand to pull back on how frequently we toss God's name into the equation when our thoughts and desires are not necessarily His.

See, having a foul mouth is more than just swearing. It includes saying anything that is contrary to God's truth. One of Satan's most subtle ways of getting dirt in our discourse is to diminish the way we view God's name and use it. Remember, Satan himself used it in vain in the Garden of Eden, introducing chaos into our world.

God's name is to be associated only with truth. When the court system was established in America, the founders introduced the requirement that the person testifying must put their hand on the Bible and swear to tell the truth, so help them God. God and truth walk hand in hand. Scripture says, "You must not swear falsely by My name, profaning the name of your God; I am Yahweh" (Leviticus 19:12). And in the book of Ezekiel, the prophet calls the people to account when he says, "Didn't you see a false vision and speak a lying divination when you proclaimed, 'This is the Lord's declaration,' even though I had not spoken?" (Ezekiel 13:7). A similar statement is made in chapter 22, verse 28: "Her prophets plaster with whitewash for them by seeing false visions and lying divinations, and they say, 'This is what the Lord GOD says,' when the LORD has not spoken."

To use God's name in vain is profane. It is profanity. It's easy to recognize profanity when someone is swearing, but it's not so easy to recognize it when someone attaches God's name to something He did not declare. Even though we may not swear with curse words, we are using profanity when we use God's name illegitimately. Knowing this, it would be wise to watch your mouth before telling anyone that God told you to do this, that, or the other.

Curses

Cursing isn't just about bad language. When you tell someone to "go to hell," you're pronouncing a curse on them with your language. A curse in the Bible is a pronouncement of evil, judgment, or ruin on a person. You are damning them. This is similar to what we studied earlier when Jesus saw the fig tree not producing and cursed it so that it would no longer bear fruit. Jesus didn't address the tree with foul language as we understand foul language. Rather, He used His words to call for its ruin. That's why we have to understand that when we use our words in a derogatory manner toward someone else or toward God, we are pronouncing a curse. We are speaking death into their lives.

Never take the power of your speech lightly—even when it's taken lightly in our culture. Turn on practically any afternoon talk show on television, and you will hear people cursing each other up one side and down the other. They may or may not be swearing, but they are speaking words of destruction, accusation, judgment, and death. That is profanity, and it should not come from the mouth of a child of the holy and righteous King. We read in the book of Psalms what can happen to the one who speaks death to another.

> He loved cursing—let it fall on him;
> he took no delight in blessing—let it be far from him.
> He wore cursing like his coat—
> let it enter his body like water
> and go into his bones like oil.
> Let it be like a robe he wraps around himself,

like a belt he always wears.
Let this be the LORD's payment to my accusers,
to those who speak evil against me (Psalm 109:17-20).

Speaking badly about others often brings ruin to yourself.

Speaking badly about others often brings ruin to yourself. When you curse others, you invite a curse on yourself. Think about that the next time you open your mouth. Do you really want to invite ruin on your own life? Are those words you're about to say worth it? This is why the apostle Peter exhorts us to pay back evil with a blessing. Peter says when you do that, the blessing you give will boomerang back to you (1 Peter 3:9).

The body of Christ is experiencing a demonic infiltration into our speech through the corruption of our mouths. Satan has no problem doing his work while using the name of God. He doesn't care that you clock in at church on Sunday as long as he's got access to your mouth by lunchtime. When Satan can influence you to use your mouth against others, he's got you right where he wants you because he knows your destructive words will come back on you.

Speaking in an unwholesome manner produces another damaging result: It damages your fellowship with the Holy Spirit. We looked at Ephesians 4:29 earlier in this chapter. In the next verse, Paul reveals the impact that unwholesome speech has on our relationship with God: "Don't grieve God's Holy Spirit. You were sealed by Him for the day of redemption."

To grieve the Holy Spirit is to sadden or offend Him. When we use language that is not edifying but rather is foul, we offend God's Spirit within us. What happens when the Spirit is grieved? The Holy Spirit is often compared to a dove in Scripture. A dove is a very sensitive bird. It will fly off quickly when you get too close because it is so sensitive. Similarly, when we grieve the Holy Spirit, we create relational distance. We limit our experience of intimacy with Him, and we limit our access to His power in our lives.

The Holy Spirit will not hang around foul language. If you want a greater experience of His influence in your life, keep Him close. One way you keep Him close is by watching your mouth. Keep in mind that this has nothing to do with your salvation. But it has everything to do with your relational intimacy with God.

I want to look briefly at a story found in Isaiah 6. Let's read the entire section first.

> In the year that King Uzziah died, I saw the Lord seated on a high and lofty throne, and His robe filled the temple. Seraphim were standing above Him; each one had six wings: with two he covered his face, with two he covered his feet, and with two he flew. And one called to another:
>> Holy, holy, holy is the LORD of Hosts;
>> His glory fills the whole earth.
> The foundations of the doorways shook at the sound of their voices, and the temple was filled with smoke.
> Then I said:
>> Woe is me for I am ruined
>> because I am a man of unclean lips
>> and live among a people of unclean lips,
>> and because my eyes have seen the King,
>> the LORD of Hosts.
> Then one of the seraphim flew to me, and in his

hand was a glowing coal that he had taken from the altar
with tongs. He touched my mouth with it and said:

> Now that this has touched your lips,
> your wickedness is removed
> and your sin is atoned for.

Then I heard the voice of the Lord saying:

> Who should I send?
> Who will go for Us?

I said:

> Here I am. Send me (Isaiah 6:1-8).

During a period of deep distress, Isaiah was ushered into the presence of the Lord. Only when he came face-to-face with the purity
of God's glory did he realize his own impurity. He refers to himself
as "ruined" and having "unclean lips." Not only that, but Isaiah confesses that those he lives alongside are also plagued with "unclean lips."

Friend, having unclean lips is no small thing. After Isaiah's confession, God instructed a seraphim to touch his mouth with a coal in
order to remove the wickedness from his words. The lips are extremely
sensitive, so the process of transforming Isaiah's speech was very painful for him. However, this process cleansed him through his repen-
tance, and it empowered him to hear God's voice anew and get clarity
on the direction he was to take going forward.

Dealing with your tongue may be a painful process, but it will be
worth it.

Speech is a powerful force—one we should never take lightly. Dirt
in your discourse affects not only those who are listening to you but
also yourself. Make it your intention to use your mouth wisely and
watch God move in your life in ways you never could have dreamed.

Conclusion

In the southern part of Turkey there are cranes that are known for the loud squawking sound they make when they fly. However, the sound often attracts eagles that attack young cranes. Mature cranes, aware of the danger, keep a stone in their mouths when they fly so the squawking cannot be heard. They demonstrate the message of this book—life and death are determined by what comes out of your mouth.

The apostle Paul addresses the issue of our speech when he says, "Don't give the Devil an opportunity" (Ephesians 4:27). Just as the eagles listen for the sound of cranes, our spiritual adversary is intently attuned to the sounds coming out of our mouths. He is keenly aware that if our speech is full of cursing, negative self-talk, and unwholesome speech, the door has been opened for him to wreak havoc in our lives and in the lives of others. Conversely, if we fill our mouths with hopeful, healing, and wholesome speech rooted in God's Word, then like the mature cranes, we will thwart the enemy and bring blessing to our lives and to the lives of others.

Scripture declares that Satan is like a roaring lion, looking for anyone he can devour (1 Peter 5:8). We must make sure that our words are not serving as an open invitation for our enemy to devour us. Satan uses the door of mouths as a major entryway into the rest of our lives, and we must be vigilant with the words we use.

So make it your mission to use your mouth to speak blessings and not curses. Bless your family around the dinner table, encourage your mate regularly in your marriage, speak life and not death to your friends and enemies alike. And if speaking the truth requires you to say something challenging to someone, make sure you communicate your positive desire that the truth you speak will set them free.

May we all learn and utilize the lesson of the cranes and take seriously the injunction, watch your mouth.

What the Bible Says About Our Words

The Wise Tongue

Proverbs

For the LORD gives wisdom; from His mouth come knowledge and understanding (2:6).

Don't rebuke a mocker, or he will hate you; rebuke a wise man, and he will love you (9:8).

Hatred stirs up conflicts, but love covers all offenses. Wisdom is found on the lips of the discerning, but a rod is for the back of the one who lacks sense (10:12-13).

The wise store up knowledge, but the mouth of the fool hastens destruction (10:14).

When there are many words, sin is unavoidable, but the one who controls his lips is wise (10:19).

There is one who speaks rashly, like a piercing sword; but the tongue of the wise brings healing (12:18).

The proud speech of a fool brings a rod of discipline, but the lips of the wise protect them (14:3).

The tongue of the wise makes knowledge attractive, but the mouth of fools blurts out foolishness (15:2).

The lips of the wise broadcast knowledge, but not so the heart of fools (15:7).

A discerning mind seeks knowledge, but the mouth of fools feeds on foolishness (15:14).

A man takes joy in giving an answer; and a timely word—how good that is! (15:23).

A wise heart instructs its mouth and increases learning with its speech (16:23).

To start a conflict is to release a flood; stop the dispute before it breaks out (17:14).

The intelligent person restrains his words, and one who keeps a cool head is a man of understanding. Even a fool is considered wise when he keeps silent, discerning when he seals his lips (17:27-28).

There is gold and a multitude of jewels, but knowledgeable lips are a rare treasure (20:15).

The one who guards his mouth and tongue keeps himself out of trouble (21:23).

Listen closely, pay attention to the words of the wise, and apply your mind to my knowledge. For it is pleasing if you keep them within you and if they are constantly on your lips (22:17-18).

A word spoken at the right time is like gold apples on a silver tray (25:11).

A wise correction to a receptive ear is like a gold ring or an ornament of gold (25:12).

A fool gives full vent to his anger, but a wise man holds it in check (29:11).

She opens her mouth with wisdom and loving instruction is on her tongue (31:26).

Ecclesiastes

Do not be hasty to speak, and do not be impulsive to make a speech before God. God is in heaven and you are on earth, so let your words be few (5:2).

The words from the mouth of a wise man are gracious, but the lips of a fool consume him (10:12).

The Foolish Tongue

Proverbs

The wise store up knowledge, but the mouth of the fool hastens destruction (10:14).

The lips of the righteous feed many, but fools die for lack of sense (10:21).

Whoever shows contempt for his neighbor lacks sense, but a man with understanding keeps silent (11:12).

A fool's displeasure is known at once, but whoever ignores an insult is sensible (12:16).

A shrewd person conceals knowledge, but a foolish heart publicizes stupidity (12:23).

The one who guards his mouth protects his life; the one who opens his lips invites his own ruin (13:3).

The proud speech of a fool brings a rod of discipline, but the lips of the wise protect them (14:3).

Stay away from a foolish man; you will gain no knowledge from his speech (14:7).

The tongue of the wise makes knowledge attractive, but the mouth of fools blurts out foolishness (15:2).

A discerning mind seeks knowledge, but the mouth of fools feeds on foolishness (15:14).

Even a fool is considered wise when he keeps silent, discerning when he seals his lips (17:28).

A fool does not delight in understanding, but only wants to show off his opinions (18:2).

A fool's lips lead to strife, and his mouth provokes a beating. A fool's mouth is his devastation, and his lips are a trap for his life (18:6-7).

The one who gives an answer before he listens—this is foolishness and disgrace for him (18:13).

Differing weights are detestable to the Lord, and dishonest scales are unfair (20:23).

A fool gives full vent to his anger, but a wise man holds it in check (29:11).

Do you see a man who speaks too soon? There is more hope for a fool than for him (29:20).

The Hurtful Tongue

Proverbs

You have been trapped by the words of your lips—ensnared by the words of your mouth (6:2).

A man will be satisfied with good by the words of his mouth, and the work of a man's hands will reward him (12:14).

From the words of his mouth, a man will enjoy good things, but treacherous people have an appetite for violence (13:2).

A gentle answer turns away anger, but a harsh word stirs up wrath (15:1).

The tongue that heals is a tree of life, but a devious tongue breaks the spirit (15:4).

Life and death are in the power of the tongue, and those who love it will eat its fruit (18:21).

Better to live on the corner of a roof than to share a house with a nagging wife (21:9).

Better to live in a wilderness than with a nagging and hot-tempered wife (21:19).

Don't envy evil men or desire to be with them, for their hearts plan violence, and their words stir up trouble (24:12).

The Helpful Tongue

Proverbs

Anxiety in a man's heart weighs it down, but a good word cheers it up (12:25).

A gentle answer turns away anger, but a harsh word stirs up wrath (15:1).

The tongue that heals is a tree of life, but a devious tongue breaks the spirit (15:4).

A man takes joy in giving an answer; and a timely word—how good that is! (15:23).

The LORD detests the plans of an evil man, but pleasant words are pure (15:26).

Anyone with a wise heart is called discerning, and pleasant speech increases learning (16:21).

Pleasant words are a honeycomb: sweet to the taste and health to the body (16:24).

The one who guards his mouth and tongue keeps himself out of trouble (21:23).

The one who loves a pure heart and gracious lips—the king is his friend (22:11).

A word spoken at the right time is like gold apples on a silver tray (25:11).

One who rebukes a person will later find more favor than one who flatters with his tongue (28:23).

Speak up for those who have no voice, for the justice of all who are dispossessed. Speak up, judge righteously, and defend the cause of the oppressed and needy (31:8-9).

2 Corinthians

Praise the God and Father of our Lord Jesus Christ, the Father of mercies and the God of all comfort. He comforts us in all our affliction, so that we may be able to comfort those who are in any kind of affliction, through the comfort we ourselves receive from God (1:3-4).

Ephesians

But speaking the truth in love, let us grow in every way into Him who is the head—Christ (4:15).

No foul language is to come from your mouth, but only what is good for building up someone in need, so that it gives grace to those who hear (4:29).

Colossians

Your speech should always be gracious, seasoned with salt, so that you may know how you should answer each person (4:6).

1 Thessalonians

Therefore encourage one another and build each other up as you are already doing (5:11).

And we exhort you, brothers: warn those who are irresponsible, comfort the discouraged, help the weak, be patient with everyone (5:14).

Hebrews

But encourage each other daily, while it is still called today, so that none of you is hardened by sin's deception (3:13).

1 Peter

Not paying back evil for evil or insult for insult but, on the contrary, giving a blessing, since you were called for this, so that you can inherit a blessing (3:9).

The Indecent Tongue

Psalms

He loved cursing—let it fall on him; he took no delight in blessing—let it be far from him. He wore cursing like his coat—let it enter his body like water and go into his bones like oil (109:17-18).

Proverbs

The mouth of the righteous produces wisdom, but a perverse tongue will be cut out (10:31).

The lips of the righteous know what is appropriate, but the mouth of the wicked, only what is perverse (10:32).

An evil man is trapped by his rebellious speech, but a righteous one escapes from trouble (12:13).

Ecclesiastes

Do not curse the king even in your thoughts, and do not curse a rich person even in your bedroom, for a bird of the sky may carry the message, and a winged creature may report the matter (10:20).

Ephesians

No foul language is to come from your mouth, but only what is good for building up someone in need, so that it gives grace to those who hear (4:29).

But sexual immorality and any impurity or greed should not even be heard of among you, as is proper for saints. Coarse and foolish talking or crude joking are not suitable, but rather giving thanks (5:3-4).

The Boastful Tongue

Psalms

For the wicked one boasts about his own cravings; the one who is greedy curses and despises the LORD (10:3).

Proverbs

Let another praise you, and not your own mouth—a stranger, and not your own lips (27:2).

If you have been foolish by exalting yourself or if you've been scheming, put your hand over your mouth (30:32).

Jeremiah

This is what the LORD says: The wise man must not boast in his wisdom; the strong man must not boast in his strength; the wealthy man must not boast in his wealth. But the one who boasts should boast in this, that he understands and knows Me—that I am Yahweh, showing faithful love, justice, and righteousness on the earth, for I delight in these things. This is the LORD's declaration (9:23-24).

2 Corinthians

For we don't dare classify or compare ourselves with some who commend themselves. But in measuring themselves by themselves and comparing themselves to themselves, they lack understanding (10:12).

So the one who boasts must boast in the Lord. For it is not the one commending himself who is approved, but the one the Lord commends (10:17-18).

2 Timothy

For people will be lovers of self, lovers of money, boastful, proud, blasphemers, disobedient to parents, ungrateful, unholy (3:2).

James

Come now, you who say, "Today or tomorrow we will travel to such and such a city and spend a year there and do business and make a profit." You don't even know what tomorrow will bring—what your life will be! For you are like smoke that appears for a little while, then vanishes. Instead, you should say, "If the Lord wills, we will live and do this or that." But as it is, you boast in your arrogance. All such boasting is evil. So it is a sin for the person who knows to do what is good and doesn't do it (4:13-17).

The Gossiping Tongue

Proverbs

A gossip goes around revealing a secret, but a trustworthy person keeps a confidence (11:13).

A contrary man spreads conflict, and a gossip separates close friends (16:28).

Whoever conceals an offense promotes love, but whoever gossips about it separates friends (17:9).

A gossip's words are like choice food that goes down to one's innermost being (18:8).

The one who reveals secrets is a constant gossip; avoid someone with a big mouth (20:19).

Romans

They are filled with all unrighteousness, evil, greed, and wickedness. They are full of envy, murder, quarrels, deceit, and malice. They are gossips, slanderers, God-haters, arrogant, proud, boastful, inventors of evil, disobedient to parents (1:29-30).

2 Corinthians

For I fear that perhaps when I come I will not find you to be what I want, and I may not be found by you to be what you want; there may be quarreling, jealousy, outbursts of anger, selfish ambitions, slander, gossip, arrogance, and disorder (12:20).

1 Timothy

At the same time, they also learn to be idle, going from house to house; they are not only idle, but are also gossips and busybodies, saying things they shouldn't say (5:13).

The Slanderous Tongue

Psalms

LORD, who can dwell in Your tent? Who can live on Your holy mountain? The one who lives honestly, practices righteousness, and acknowledges the truth in his heart—who does not slander with his tongue, who does not harm his friend or discredit his neighbor (15:1-3).

Do not let a slanderer stay in the land. Let evil relentlessly hunt down a violent man (140:11).

Proverbs

The one who conceals hatred has lying lips, and whoever spreads slander is a fool (10:18).

A gossip goes around revealing a secret, but a trustworthy person keeps a confidence (11:13).

The one who reveals secrets is a constant gossip; avoid someone with a big mouth (20:19).

Don't testify against your neighbor without cause. Don't deceive with your lips (24:28).

A gossip's words are like choice food that goes down to one's innermost being (26:22).

1 Corinthians

But now I am writing you not to associate with anyone who claims to be a believer who is sexually immoral or greedy, an idolater or verbally abusive, a drunkard or a swindler. Do not even eat with such a person (5:11).

James

But He gives greater grace. Therefore He says: God resists the proud, but gives grace to the humble (4:6).

The Deceptive Tongue

Job

I will be partial to no one, and I will not give anyone an undeserved title. For I do not know how to give such titles; otherwise, my Maker would remove me in an instant (32:21-22).

Psalms

For there is nothing reliable in what they say; destruction is within them; their throat is an open grave; they flatter with their tongues (5:9).

May the LORD cut off all flattering lips and the tongue that speaks boastfully (12:3).

"LORD, deliver me from lying lips and a deceitful tongue." What will He give you, and what will He do to you, you deceitful tongue? (120:2-3).

Proverbs

Don't let your mouth speak dishonestly, and don't let your lips talk deviously (4:24).

The LORD hates six things; in fact, seven are detestable to Him: arrogant eyes, a lying tongue, hands that shed innocent blood, a heart that plots wicked schemes, feet eager to run to evil, a lying witness who gives false testimony, and one who stirs up trouble among brothers (6:16-19).

The one who conceals hatred has lying lips, and whoever spreads slander is a fool (10:18).

The mouth of the righteous produces wisdom, but a perverse tongue will be cut out (10:31).

Whoever speaks the truth declares what is right, but a false witness, deceit (12:17).

Truthful lips endure forever, but a lying tongue, only a moment (12:19).

Lying lips are detestable to the LORD, but faithful people are His delight (12:22).

A wicked person listens to malicious talk; a liar pays attention to a destructive tongue (17:4).

One with a twisted mind will not succeed, and one with deceitful speech will fall into ruin (17:20).

Better a poor man who lives with integrity than someone who has deceitful lips and is a fool (19:1).

A false witness will not go unpunished, and one who utters lies will not escape (19:5).

Making a fortune through a lying tongue is a vanishing mist, a pursuit of death (21:6).

Like a madman who throws flaming darts and deadly arrows, so is the man who deceives his neighbor and says, "I was only joking!" (26:18-19).

Smooth lips with an evil heart are like glaze on an earthen vessel. A hateful person disguises himself with his speech and harbors deceit within. When he speaks graciously, don't believe him, for there are seven abominations in his heart (26:23-25).

A lying tongue hates those it crushes and a flattering mouth causes ruin (26:28).

Isaiah

Indeed, the LORD's hand is not too short to save, and His ear is not too deaf to hear. But your iniquities have built barriers between you and your God, and your sins have made Him hide His face from you so that He does not listen. For your hands are defiled with blood and your fingers, with iniquity; your lips have spoken lies, and your tongues mutter injustice (59:1-3).

James

If anyone thinks he is religious without controlling his tongue, then his religion is useless and he deceives himself (1:26).

1 Peter

For the one who wants to love life and to see good days must keep his tongue from evil and his lips from speaking deceit (3:10).

Jude

These people are discontented grumblers, walking according to their desires; their mouths utter arrogant words, flattering people for their own advantage (16).

The Wicked Tongue

Exodus

Do not misuse the name of the LORD your God, because the LORD will not leave anyone unpunished who misuses His name (20:7).

Psalms

Cursing, deceit, and violence fill his mouth; trouble and malice are under his tongue (10:7).

LORD, I seek refuge in You; let me never be disgraced. Save me by Your righteousness (31:1).

For You are my rock and my fortress; You lead and guide me because of Your name (31:3).

Keep your tongue from evil and your lips from deceitful speech (34:13).

Like a sharpened razor, your tongue devises destruction, working treachery (52:2).

Proverbs

A worthless person, a wicked man goes around speaking dishonestly, winking his eyes, signaling with his feet, and gesturing with his fingers. He always plots evil with perversity in his heart—he stirs up trouble (6:12-14).

The mouth of the righteous is a fountain of life, but the mouth of the wicked conceals violence. Hatred stirs up conflicts, but love covers all offenses. Wisdom is found on the lips of the discerning, but a rod is for the back of the one who lacks sense (10:11-13).

The tongue of the righteous is pure silver; the heart of the wicked is of little value (10:20).

The lips of the righteous know what is appropriate, but the mouth of the wicked, only what is perverse (10:32).

A city is built up by the blessing of the upright, but it is torn down by the mouth of the wicked (11:11).

An evil man is trapped by his rebellious speech, but a righteous one escapes from trouble (12:13).

The one who guards his mouth protects his life; the one who opens his lips invites his own ruin (13:3).

The mind of the righteous person thinks before answering, but the mouth of the wicked blurts out evil things (15:28).

A worthless man digs up evil, and his speech is like a scorching fire (16:27).

A worthless witness mocks justice, and a wicked mouth swallows iniquity (19:28).

Ecclesiastes

Do not let your mouth bring guilt on you, and do not say in the presence of the messenger that it was a mistake. Why should God be angry with your words and destroy the work of your hands? (5:6).

Ezekiel

Didn't you see a false vision and speak a lying divination when you proclaimed, 'This is the LORD's declaration,' even though I had not spoken? (13:7).

Her prophets plaster with whitewash for them by seeing false visions and lying divinations, and they say, 'This is what the Lord GOD says,' when the LORD has not spoken (22:28).

Matthew

"Are even you still lacking in understanding?" He asked. "Don't you realize that whatever goes into the mouth passes into the stomach and is eliminated? But what comes out of the mouth comes from the heart, and this defiles a man. For from the heart come evil thoughts, murders, adulteries, sexual immoralities, thefts, false testimonies, blasphemies. These are the things that defile a man, but eating with unwashed hands does not defile a man" (15:16-20).

Romans

Therefore, any one of you who judges is without excuse. For when you judge another, you condemn yourself, since you, the judge, do the same things (2:1).

Their throat is an open grave; they deceive with their tongues. Vipers' venom is under their lips. Their mouth is full of cursing and bitterness (3:13-14).

Ephesians

Coarse and foolish talking or crude joking are not suitable, but rather giving thanks (5:4).

2 Timothy

But avoid irreverent, empty speech, for this will produce an even greater measure of godlessness (2:16).

The Godly Tongue

Psalms

Lord, who can dwell in Your tent? Who can live on Your holy mountain? The one who lives honestly, practices righteousness, and acknowledges the truth in his heart who does not slander with his tongue, who does not harm his friend or discredit his neighbor (15:1-3).

You have tested my heart; You have examined me at night. You have tried me and found nothing evil; I have determined that my mouth will not sin (17:3).

May the words of my mouth and the meditation of my heart be acceptable to You, Lord, my rock and my Redeemer (19:14).

I said, "I will guard my ways so that I may not sin with my tongue; I will guard my mouth with a muzzle as long as the wicked are in my presence" (39:1).

Let the redeemed of the Lord proclaim that He has redeemed them from the hand of the foe (107:2).

With my lips I proclaim all the judgments from Your mouth (119:13).

Before a word is on my tongue, You know all about it, Lord (139:4).

Lord, set up a guard for my mouth; keep watch at the door of my lips (141:3).

Proverbs

For my mouth tells the truth, and wickedness is detestable to my lips. All the words of my mouth are righteous; none of them are deceptive or perverse (8:7-8).

The tongue of the righteous is pure silver; the heart of the wicked is of little value (10:20).

Whoever speaks the truth declares what is right, but a false witness, deceit (12:17).

Truthful lips endure forever, but a lying tongue, only a moment (12:19).

Lying lips are detestable to the LORD, but faithful people are His delight (12:22).

Isaiah

Then I said: "Woe is me for I am ruined because I am a man of unclean lips and live among a people of unclean lips, and because my eyes have seen the King, the LORD of Hosts." Then one of the seraphim flew to me, and in his hand was a glowing coal that he had taken from the altar with tongs. He touched my mouth with it and said: "Now that this has touched your lips, your wickedness is removed and your sin is atoned for" (6:5-7).

Malachi

True instruction was in his mouth, and nothing wrong was found on his lips. He walked with Me in peace and fairness and turned many from sin (2:6).

Mark

So when they arrest you and hand you over, don't worry beforehand what you will say. On the contrary, whatever is given to you in that hour—say it. For it isn't you speaking, but the Holy Spirit (13:11).

James

My dearly loved brothers, understand this: Everyone must be quick to hear, slow to speak, and slow to anger, for man's anger does not accomplish God's righteousness (1:19-20).

1 Peter

For the one who wants to love life and to see good days must keep his tongue from evil and his lips from speaking deceit (3:10).

The Powerful Tongue

2 Chronicles

"Tomorrow, go down against them. You will see them coming up the Ascent of Ziz, and you will find them at the end of the valley facing the Wilderness of Jeruel. You do not have to fight this battle. Position yourselves, stand still, and see the salvation of the LORD. He is with you, Judah and Jerusalem. Do not be afraid or discouraged. Tomorrow, go out to face them, for Yahweh is with you."

Then Jehoshaphat bowed with his face to the ground, and all Judah and the inhabitants of Jerusalem fell down before the LORD to worship Him. Then the Levites from the sons of the Kohathites and the Korahites stood up to praise the LORD God of Israel shouting with a loud voice.

In the morning they got up early and went out to the wilderness of Tekoa. As they were about to go out, Jehoshaphat stood and said, "Hear me, Judah and you inhabitants of Jerusalem. Believe in Yahweh your God, and you will be established; believe in His prophets, and you will succeed." Then he consulted with the people and appointed some to sing for the LORD and some to praise the splendor of His holiness. When they went out in front of the armed forces, they kept singing:

"Give thanks to the LORD,
   for His faithful love endures forever."

The moment they began their shouts and praises, the LORD set
an ambush against the Ammonites, Moabites, and the inhabitants of Mount Seir who came to fight against Judah, and they were
defeated (20:16-22).

Proverbs

You have been trapped by the words of your lips—ensnared by the
words of your mouth (6:2).

Whoever speaks the truth declares what is right, but a false witness,
deceit. There is one who speaks rashly, like a piercing sword; but the
tongue of the wise brings healing. Truthful lips endure forever, but a
lying tongue, only a moment (12:17-19).

Life and death are in the power of the tongue, and those who love it
will eat its fruit (18:21).

Isaiah

This is what the LORD, the Holy One of Israel and its Maker, says:
"Ask Me what is to happen to My sons, and instruct Me about the
work of My hands" (45:11).

Even before they call, I will answer; while they are still speaking, I will
hear (65:24).

Matthew

Brood of vipers! How can you speak good things when you are evil?
For the mouth speaks from the overflow of the heart. A good man
produces good things from his storeroom of good, and an evil man
produces evil things from his storeroom of evil. I tell you that on the

day of judgment people will have to account for every careless word they speak. For by your words you will be acquitted, and by your words you will be condemned (12:34-37).

Mark

Then Peter remembered and said to Him, "Rabbi, look! The fig tree that You cursed is withered." Jesus replied to them, "Have faith in God. I assure you: If anyone says to this mountain, 'Be lifted up and thrown into the sea,' and does not doubt in his heart, but believes that what he says will happen, it will be done for him. Therefore I tell you, all the things you pray and ask for—believe that you have received them, and you will have them" (11:21-24).

Luke

A good man produces good out of the good storeroom of his heart. An evil man produces evil out of the evil storeroom, for his mouth speaks from the overflow of the heart (6:45).

Romans

If you confess with your mouth, "Jesus is Lord," and believe in your heart that God raised Him from the dead, you will be saved. One believes with the heart, resulting in righteousness, and one confesses with the mouth, resulting in salvation (10:9-10).

So faith comes from what is heard, and what is heard comes through the message about Christ (10:17).

2 Corinthians

And since we have the same spirit of faith in keeping with what is written, I believed, therefore I spoke, we also believe, and therefore speak (4:13).

Hebrews

Since it remains for some to enter it, and those who formerly received the good news did not enter because of disobedience (4:16).

Your life should be free from the love of money. Be satisfied with what you have, for He Himself has said, I will never leave you or forsake you. Therefore, we may boldly say: The Lord is my helper; I will not be afraid. What can man do to me? (13:5-6).

1 John

Now this is the confidence we have before Him: Whenever we ask anything according to His will, He hears us. And if we know that He hears whatever we ask, we know that we have what we have asked Him for (5:14-15).

The Praising Tongue

2 Chronicles

Then the Levites from the sons of the Kohathites and the Korahites stood up to praise the LORD God of Israel shouting with a loud voice. In the morning they got up early and went out to the wilderness of Tekoa. As they were about to go out, Jehoshaphat stood and said, "Hear me, Judah and you inhabitants of Jerusalem. Believe in Yahweh your God, and you will be established; believe in His prophets, and you will succeed." Then he consulted with the people and appointed some to sing for the LORD and some to praise the splendor of His holiness. When they went out in front of the armed forces, they kept singing: "Give thanks to the LORD, for His faithful love endures forever." The moment they began their shouts and praises, the LORD set an ambush against the Ammonites, Moabites, and the inhabitants of Mount Seir who came to fight against Judah, and they were defeated (20:19-22).

Psalms

You are holy, enthroned on the praises of Israel (22:3).

I will praise the LORD at all times; His praise will always be on my lips. I will boast in the LORD; the humble will hear and be glad. Proclaim Yahweh's greatness with me; let us exalt His name together (34:1-3).

And my tongue will proclaim Your righteousness, Your praise all day long (35:28).

Whoever sacrifices a thank offering honors Me, and whoever orders his conduct, I will show him the salvation of God (50:23).

Shout joyfully to God, all the earth! Sing about the glory of His name; make His praise glorious. Say to God, "How awe-inspiring are Your works! Your enemies will cringe before You because of Your great strength. All the earth will worship You and sing praise to You. They will sing praise to Your name" (66:1-4).

I cried out to Him with my mouth, and praise was on my tongue (66:17).

Let the peoples praise You, God, let all the peoples praise You. The earth has produced its harvest; God, our God, blesses us (67:5-6).

Therefore, my tongue will proclaim Your righteousness all day long, for those who seek my harm will be disgraced and confounded (71:24).

Enter His gates with thanksgiving and His courts with praise. Give thanks to Him and praise His name (100:4).

My tongue sings about Your promise, for all Your commands are righteous (119:172).

Let the exaltation of God be in their mouths and a double-edged sword in their hands, inflicting vengeance on the nations and punishment on the peoples, binding their kings with chains and their dignitaries with iron shackles, carrying out the judgment decreed against them. This honor is for all His godly people. Hallelujah! (149:6-9).

Isaiah

Violence will never again be heard of in your land; devastation and destruction will be gone from your borders. But you will name your walls salvation and your gates, praise (60:18).

Hebrews

Therefore, through Him let us continually offer up to God a sacrifice of praise, that is, the fruit of our lips that confess His name (13:15).

Appendix 2

Dr. Tony Evans and The Urban Alternative

About Dr. Tony Evans

Dr. Tony Evans is founder and senior pastor of the 10,000-member Oak Cliff Bible Fellowship in Dallas, founder and president of The Urban Alternative, chaplain of the NBA's Dallas Mavericks, and author of many books, including *Destiny* and *Victory in Spiritual Warfare*. His radio broadcast, *The Alternative with Dr. Tony Evans*, can be heard on more than 1000 outlets and in more than 100 countries.

The Urban Alternative

The Urban Alternative (TUA) equips, empowers, and unites Christians to impact individuals, families, churches, and communities. TUA promotes a worldview that is thoroughly based on God's kingdom agenda. In teaching truth, we seek to transform lives.

The root of the problems we face in our personal lives, homes, churches, and societies is a spiritual one; therefore, the only way to address it is spiritually. We've tried political, social, economic, and religious agendas, but they have not brought lasting transformation.

It's time for a kingdom agenda—the visible manifestation of the comprehensive rule of God over every area of life.

The unifying, central theme of the Bible is the glory of God through the advancement of His kingdom. This is the conjoining thread from Genesis to Revelation—from beginning to end. Without that theme, the Bible is a disconnected collection of stories that are inspiring but seem to be unrelated in purpose and direction. The Bible exists to share God's movement in history toward the establishment and expansion of His kingdom, highlighting the connectivity throughout which is the kingdom. This understanding increases the relevancy of these ancient writings to our day-to-day living because the kingdom is not only then; it is now.

The absence of the kingdom's influence in our own lives and in our families, churches, and communities has led to a catastrophic deterioration in our world.

- People live segmented, compartmentalized lives because they lack God's kingdom worldview.

- Families disintegrate because they exist for their own satisfaction rather than for the kingdom.

- Churches have limited impact because they fail to comprehend that the goal of the church is not the church itself, but the kingdom.

- Communities have nowhere to turn to find real solutions for real people who have real problems because the church has become divided, ingrown, and powerless to transform the cultural landscape in any relevant way.

The kingdom agenda offers us a way to live with a solid hope by optimizing the solutions of heaven. When God and His rule are not the final and authoritative standard over all, order and hope are lost. But the reverse is true as well—as long as we have God, we have hope. If God is still in the picture, and as long as His agenda is still on the table, it's not over.

Even if relationships collapse, God will sustain you. Even if finances dwindle, God will keep you. Even if dreams die, God will revive you. As long as God and His rule guide your life, family, church, and community, there is always hope.

Our world needs the King's agenda. Our churches need the King's agenda. Our families need the King's agenda.

In many major cities, drivers can take a loop to get to the other side of the city without driving straight through downtown. This loop takes them close enough to the city to see its towering buildings and skyline, but not close enough to actually experience it.

This is precisely what our culture has done with God. We have put Him on the "loop" of our personal, family, church, and community lives. He's close enough to be at hand should we need Him in an emergency, but too far away to be the center of who we are.

Sadly, we often want God on the "loop" of our lives, but we don't always want the King of the Bible to come downtown into the very heart of our ways. Leaving God on the "loop" brings about dire consequences, as we have seen in our own lives and with others. But when we make God and His rule the centerpiece of all we think, do, and say, we experience Him in the way He longs for us to.

He wants us to be kingdom people with kingdom minds set on fulfilling His kingdom purposes. He wants us to pray as Jesus did— "Not my will, but Thy will be done." Because His is the kingdom, the power, and the glory.

There is only one God, and we are not Him. As King and Creator, God calls the shots. Only when we align ourselves underneath His comprehensive hand will we access His full power and authority in our lives, families, churches, and communities.

As we learn how to govern ourselves under God, we will transform the institutions of family, church, and society according to a biblically based, kingdom worldview.

Under Him, we touch heaven and change earth.

To achieve our goal, we use a variety of strategies, approaches, and resources for reaching and equipping as many people as possible.

Broadcast Media

Millions of individuals experience *The Alternative with Dr. Tony Evans*, a daily broadcast playing on nearly 1000 radio outlets and in more than 100 countries. The broadcast can also be seen on several television networks, online at TonyEvans.org, and on the free Tony Evans app. More than four million message downloads occur each year.

Leadership Training

The *Tony Evans Training Center (TETC)* facilitates educational programming that embodies the ministry philosophy of Dr. Tony Evans as expressed through the kingdom agenda. The training courses focus on leadership development and discipleship in five tracks:

- Bible and theology
- personal growth
- family and relationships
- church health and leadership development
- society and community impact

The TETC program includes courses for both local and online students. Furthermore, TETC programming includes course work for nonstudent attendees. Pastors, Christian leaders, and Christian laity, both local and at a distance, can seek out the Kingdom Agenda Certificate for personal, spiritual, and professional development. Some courses qualify for continuing education credits and will transfer for college credit with our partner schools.

Kingdom Agenda Pastors (KAP) provides a viable network for like-minded pastors who embrace the kingdom agenda philosophy. Pastors have the opportunity to go deeper with Dr. Tony Evans as they are given greater biblical knowledge, practical applications, and resources to impact individuals, families, churches, and communities. KAP welcomes senior and associate pastors of all churches. KAP also offers an annual summit held each year in Dallas with intensive seminars, workshops, and resources.

Pastors' Wives Ministry, founded by Dr. Lois Evans, provides counsel, encouragement, and spiritual resources for pastors' wives as they serve with their husbands in the ministry. A primary focus of the ministry is the KAP Summit, which offers senior pastors' wives a safe place to reflect, renew, and relax along with training in personal development, spiritual growth, and care for their emotional and physical well-being.

Community Impact

National Church Adopt-A-School Initiative (NCAASI) empowers churches across the country to impact communities by using public schools as the primary vehicles for effecting positive social change in urban youth and families. Leaders of churches, school districts, faith-based organizations, and other nonprofit organizations are equipped with the knowledge and tools to forge partnerships and build strong social service delivery systems. This training is based on the comprehensive church-based community impact strategy conducted by Oak Cliff Bible Fellowship. It addresses such areas as economic development, education, housing, health revitalization, family renewal, and racial reconciliation. We assist churches in tailoring the model to meet specific needs of their communities while simultaneously addressing the spiritual and moral frame of reference. Training events are held annually in the Dallas area at Oak Cliff Bible Fellowship.

Athlete's Impact (AI) is an outreach into and through sports. Coaches are sometimes the most influential adults in young people's lives—even more so than parents. With the growing rise of fatherlessness in our culture, more young people are looking to their coaches for guidance, character development, practical needs, and hope. Athletes (professional or amateur) also influence younger athletes and kids. Knowing this, we aim to equip and train coaches and athletes to live out and utilize their God-given roles for the benefit of the kingdom. We aim to do this through our iCoach App, weCoach Football Conference, and other resources, such as *The Playbook: A Life Strategy Guide for Athletes*.

Resource Development

We are fostering lifelong learning partnerships with the people we serve by providing a variety of published materials. Dr. Evans has published more than 100 unique titles (booklets, books, and Bible studies) based on more than 40 years of preaching. The goal is to strengthen individuals in their walk with God and service to others.

For more information and a complimentary copy of Dr. Evans's devotional newsletter,

call
(800) 800-3222

or write

TUA
PO Box 4000
Dallas TX 75208

or visit our website
www.TonyEvans.org

Notes

1. Sven Tagil, "Alfred Nobel's Thoughts About War and Peace," *Nobelprize.org,* http://www.nobel
   prize.org/alfred_nobel/biographical/articles/tagil/.

2. Ibid.

3. Charles Poladian, "Watch The Best Las Vegas Casino Implosions, from the Clarion to the
   Stardust," *IBT Pulse,* February 10, 2015, http://www.ibtimes.com/pulse/watch-best-las-vegas
   -casino-implosions-clarion-stardust-1811756.

More Great Harvest House Books
by Dr. Tony Evans

Watch Your Mouth Growth and Study Guide

Dr. Tony Evans says your greatest enemy is actually in your mouth. How can we control our tongues? Perfect for group or individual study, this new guide goes chapter-by-chapter through the main book, offering insightful discussion questions, Scripture, and practical application ideas to help you learn to tame your tongue.

Watch Your Mouth DVD

In this compelling DVD based on the book *Watch Your Mouth*, Dr. Tony Evans shares what the Bible teaches on the power of your words. Discover life-changing truths and practical wisdom on keeping your tongue in check. Includes four sessions—perfect for church groups or individual study.

Watch Your Mouth Interactive Workbook

In this companion to the DVD, you can follow along with Dr. Tony Evans as he shares what the Bible teaches on the power of the tongue. With this interactive workbook, you can take notes, work through insightful discussion questions, record Scripture verses, and learn practical ways to use your tongue to speak life-changing words into the world around you.

A Moment for Your Soul

In this uplifting devotional, Dr. Evans offers a daily reading for Monday through Friday and one for the weekend—all compact, powerful, and designed to reach your deepest need. Each entry includes a relevant Scripture reading for the day. (eBook only)

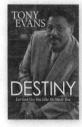

Destiny

Dr. Evans shows you the importance of finding your God-given purpose. He helps you discover and develop a custom-designed life that leads to the expansion of God's kingdom. Embracing your personal assignment from God will lead to your deepest satisfaction, God's greatest glory, and the greatest benefit to others.

It's Not Too Late

Dr. Evans uses prominent Bible characters to show that God delights in using imperfect people who have failed, sinned, or just plain blown it. You'll be encouraged as you come to understand that God has you, too, on a path to success despite your imperfections and mistakes.

The Power of God's Names

Dr. Evans shows that it's through the names of God that the nature of God is revealed. By understanding the characteristics of God as revealed through His names, you will be better equipped to face the challenges life throws at you.

Praying Through the Names of God

Dr. Evans reveals insights into some of God's powerful names and provides prayers based on those names. Your prayer life will be revitalized as you connect your needs with the relevant characteristics of His names.

Victory in Spiritual Warfare

Dr. Evans demystifies spiritual warfare and empowers you with a life-changing truth: Every struggle faced in the physical realm has its root in the spiritual realm. With passion and practicality, Dr. Evans shows you how to live a transformed life in and through the power of Christ's victory.

Prayers for Victory in Spiritual Warfare

Feel defeated? God has given you powerful weapons to help you withstand the onslaught of Satan's lies. This book of prayers, based on Dr. Evans's life-changing book *Victory in Spiritual Warfare*, will help you stand against the enemy's attacks.

30 Days to Overcoming Emotional Strongholds

Dr. Evans identifies the most common and problematic emotional strongholds and demonstrates how you can break free from them—by aligning your thoughts with God's truth in the Bible.

30 Days to Victory Through Forgiveness

Has someone betrayed you? Are you suffering the consequences of your own poor choices? Or do you find yourself asking God, *Why did You let this happen?* Like a skilled physician, Dr. Tony Evans leads you through a step-by-step remedy that will bring healing to that festering wound and get you back on your journey to your personal destiny.

Horizontal Jesus

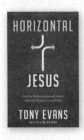

Do you want to sense God's encouragement, comfort, and love for you every day? Dr. Tony Evans reveals that as you live like a horizontal Jesus—giving these things away to others—you will personally experience them with God like never before. (Also available—*Horizontal Jesus Study Guide.*)

To learn more about Harvest House books and
to read sample chapters, visit our website:

www.harvesthousepublishers.com